Followers of Christ

Followers of Christ

The religious life and the Church

Johannes B. Metz

Translated by Thomas Linton

Burns & Oates/Paulist Press

2 55
m 569
c 1

First published in English in 1978
in Great Britain and associated territories
by Burns & Oates, 2-10 Jerdan Place, London SW6 5PT
and in the USA
by Paulist Press,
Editorial Office: 1865 Broadway, New York, NY 10023
Business Office: 545 Island Road, Ramsey, NJ 07446

First published in German in 1977 as *Zeit der Orden? Zur Mystik
und Politik der Nachfolge*
by Verlag Herder, Freiburg im Breisgau, Federal Republic of
Germany

ISBN: 0-8091-2138-7

Library of Congress
Catalog Card Number: 78-70817

Printed and bound in the
United States of America

Contents

Foreword

This book goes back to a lecture I gave at the annual meeting of an Association of Religious Superiors. In keeping with my brief I tried to deal with those ideas that are contained for contemporary religious life in the German Synod's document *Our hope: a confession of faith for our time*.

Because I do not belong to a religious order, those who do will naturally have much to overlook here and will need to make up for my lack of inside knowledge. What I say about religious orders in general necessarily blurs many distinctions, is radical, and may at times appear rather unusual. I hope that it will not be regarded as the expression of an abstract and loveless demand that is pitched too high but as a sign of hope and expectation.

The synod document I have mentioned pointedly describes the present time of being a Christian and of church life as the hour of following Christ. But this age of following Christ is in a special way the age of the religious orders. That is so not because Christians who belong to religious orders are the exclusive representatives of following Christ, but because following Christ (which is something all Christians without qualification are called to do) needs an energetic stimulus; it demands to be lived in a radical way that can plainly be observed. In this regard we have to look more closely at the religious orders, and at those who are looking for new ways of following Christ and trying to live radically without automatically finding their home in church institutions.

In expanding this text I have made it more of an approach to the question of the Church and being a Christian, but one focused on the problem of the religious orders. The subject dealt with here is not just any piece of theological research. In fact, an answer to the question how Christianity is to be identified in practice and to the question who can be described as and who can be called to be followers of Christ is more essential than ever for the cause of theology.

Münster, February 1977   *J.B. Metz*

I What is the religious life?

I What is the religious life?

I should like to begin by explaining my understanding of the religious life. It guides me in my reflections on this subject, and hence I regard it as necessary to expound it, since otherwise what I as an outsider have to say on this question will be insufficiently clear. I start with a more functional definition of the religious life with regard to Church and society *(1)*, then offer a formal and a material definition of its essential nature *(2, 3)*. From these three elements I try to draw some initial questions about and implications for the situation and the understanding of the religious life today.

1 Innovation and shock therapy

I see the functional definition of the religious life with regard to the life of both Church and society under two aspects that affect and influence one another.

Religious orders and communities have something like an innovatory function for the Church. They offer productive models for the Church as a whole in the business of growing accustomed to living in new social, economic, intellectual and cultural situations. Often they came into being as movements that started on the fringe or margin of society as it had been: at the point where social change first became noticeable and began to establish itself.

Furthermore, religious orders at the very least have a corrective rôle: the function of redressing the balance. They are a kind of shock therapy instituted by the Holy Spirit for the Church as a whole. Against the dangerous accommodations and questionable compromises that the Church as a large-scale institution can always incline to, they press for the uncompromising nature of the Gospel and of the imitation of Christ. In this sense they are the institutionalized form of a *dangerous memory* within the Church.[1]

Finally, they have arisen for the most part not so much when the Church is flourishing as when it is profoundly disorientated and unsure of itself.

I shall examine this description of function in greater detail. Over against too nicely balanced a view of things, too great a readiness to accept things as they appear, too much compromise and over against a Church very bewildered with regard to the demands and expectations of the Gospel, the religious orders recall the lack of moderation and the onesidedness that belong to a radical imitation of Christ. In this way they try to bring movement back into the life of a Church that has over-adapted itself to the world in which it lives. For their part they are attempting to resist the idea that the Gospel is something that can hardly be lived without recourse to the desperate reflex of making everything relative. They are trying continually to remind the Church that the claim of Jesus is not to be included among those things that have two sides to them — so that one could turn this claim about as one liked — for the quite simple reason that God has not got several sides to him but only one which he turned to us in Jesus. This onesidedness is for them the criterion of orthodoxy, and it makes ecclesiastical orthodoxy a hazardous venture for them.

In this sense the religious orders have very often had a salutary shock effect within the Church as a whole. Over against a wealthy Church they have upheld the case for the poverty of Jesus. In face of a triumphant Church they laid stress on the recollection of the Passion. They upset a princely Church just as much as a bourgeois one with thoughts of the second coming. When the life of the Church had come to amicable arrangements with the secular powers that be, they prodded it with the goad of apocalyptic awareness. Against the continual attempt more or less to identify the justice dealt out by State and society with God's eschatological justice they appealed passionately to the Jesus on whom no state can be built.

If I am right, the crisis of religious life is only secondarily a crisis of vocations. In my view it is primarily a *crisis of function*, caused by the absence of major specific tasks in the Church, tasks that to a certain extent cannot be handed over to others. What I mean is that if religious orders recall their historically indicated function in the Church, and apply themselves to the tasks that result from it, that action could show part of the way out of this crisis. Then perhaps the religious orders would prove attractive to the young people whose contribution they need to do justice to this function.

I append a few questions which I trust may be regarded not as the arrogant criticisms of an outsider but as the expression of his expectations.

First of all a few very general points about what may be termed the innovatory function of religious orders. This acting as productive models is something that the religious orders must do today with particular regard to the following of Christ in the Church as a whole. I shall go into this in greater detail later. All I should like to do for the moment is to tie my questions more precisely to the task of religious orders in going ahead of the Church

13

as a whole in familiarizing themselves with changes in society and with new conditions of life: and not least with new and, to begin with, for the most part marginal expressions of religious awareness.

Where today do we find in the Church marginal or fringe innovations, new departures that start on the periphery? In the German church, for instance, the religious orders seem to be those institutions that have the least contact with the groups on the fringes of our society (however problematic and ambiguous they may be), that in their own way are concerned to experiment with alternative ways of life and radical existence, and in which a latent, searching religious awareness is not seldom involved.

Surely the 'religious' above all ought to be on the trail of a religious sense and awareness that has not withered away in our enlightened world that is so thoroughly organized in rational pursuit of its goals? Ought not they to develop a feeling and an ability to discern clearly how far religion exists in our 'post-religious' age: in unassuaged hunger and thirst after righteousness, not of course just for oneself but for the others, for the victims of our historical life; unattainable yearning for meaning and impotent rebellion against the lack of meaning that breaks in upon us; mourning and grief upheld against the unacknowledged ban on the mourning, grief and sadness of a society keyed to success and victory; longing for new life and resurrection — and all this for the most part inarticulate or at least expressed in a language far, far distant from the official language of the Church? Could not and must not individual religious orders take up the work of innovation in pursuing these hints and traces of religion and helping to overcome their lack of articulateness — and also that of the Church with regard to this kind of religious feeling?

Is it really quite misguided to assume that for example

a Benedict of Nursia, who once upon a time by gathering a community of prayer around him cultivated inaccessible regions, would today call people together in the concrete deserts of our conurbations, in order to 'cultivate' them and the speechless and helpless souls immured in them through the strength of meeting together for prayer? But where today are such initiatives to be found? Who would be better authorized and in fact more duty-bound to do that than our religious orders?

Ought it not to be the religious orders who realistically and in sober perplexity make people aware of the religious crisis *within* our Church, of the growing doubt and suspicion among what may be termed the Church's lower orders, of the prevailing disappearance of internalized, serious religious conviction among even members of the Church. Surely they should continually, energetically and firmly insist on our ecclesiastical structures and the bishops at their head refusing to plan and administer their way round this development by ignoring it.

Where in our world is there really to be found today what in my view is the necessary and fruitful tension (indeed the living antagonism) between the religious orders and the institutional Church?[2] Where are the tensions that marked the early history of most religious orders, to name but two examples, in the cases of Francis of Assisi and Ignatius of Loyola?

Have not the religious orders moved too far into that middle ground where everything is nicely balanced and moderate: so to speak adapted to and tamed by the institutional Church? And is it not for this reason that they themselves have to such an extent been drawn into the general atmosphere of ecclesiastical crisis; in under that overcast pall, and into that overwhelming greyness that overshadows our ecclesiastical life today and that could and should be dispelled by an initiative from the religious orders?

Where today do the religious orders exert a shock-effect within the Church? Where are they passionately concerned to make prophetic criticism within the Church something that counts, given that because of the way in which their style of life is meant to be a close following of Christ this is something that is not just tolerated but expected of them — even if it is always difficult for genuine prophets to enter upon their task and avail themselves of it? Is the crisis in the Church to develop without any prophetic exaggeration, without any religious radicalism? If the religious orders do not become involved at this point, other prophets and other radicals will come on the stage — and have done so for a long time.

Who in the Church today withstands the danger of creeping passive adaptation to a late bourgeois mentality of prosperity? I find this adaptation much more dangerous, because it is more a matter of atmosphere and less of a definite programme, than what is termed active adaptation (by individual 'innovators'), and it affects all of us like a collective contamination. Who arouses our Church from that frozen sleep of the spirit with which it tries to resist the demands of our age without wanting to pass through them? Who finally helps to prevent a local church more and more falling apart in two pieces: a service-church for the ceremonies and festivals of bourgeois life and a church which, perhaps with reference to the saying about the 'little flock', becomes more and more, sociologically speaking, a sect — with symptoms of anxiety about coming into contact with anything strange or not understood, with syndromes of over-anxiety, with complicated defence mechanisms, with an exclusively internal system of communication, with signs of excessive loyalty and fanaticism?

Is there not, too, something like a dubious provincialism on the part of the local church that continually makes it difficult for it to measure itself by universal standards in the ecclesiastical and socio-economic fields — or, more particularly, to take into account the transformations that are emerging in the perspective of the world as a whole and to use these to provide the bearings for the judgment of its own situation as well as of the setting of its immediate and urgent goals? Inasmuch as the religious orders are often stamped with an international character and are communities intertwined on a world-wide scale, would this not provide them with an especial opportunity and task with regard to our local church to the extent that the latter, in its awareness of its situation and duties, takes its bearings all too exclusively from the internal ecclesiastical and socio-economic structure of the country? And could not, indeed should not the religious orders act as a pace-maker in the implementation of those missions of our church in the field of the Church as a whole, and society as a whole; towards the living unity of all Christians; towards a new relationship to the religious history of the Jewish people; towards a sharing of resources with the poor churches; and towards a future for mankind that would be worth living?

Here clearly there would be an abundance of corrective tasks, of tasks involving a proper balance in the Church. But are the religious orders still in a position to undertake them in the interest of the Church as a whole? Are they still willing to give their attention to such critical and therapeutic work? Or have they become too integrated into and reconciled with the institutional Church? Is there not something like a cunning strategy on the part of the institutional Church to adapt the religious orders and to reduce the tension of the antagonism between them and it? Surely the example of the growing sacerdotalization of religious orders in the Church's recent history belongs to this cunning strategy of adaptation. Is the legal exemption of religious orders (over against the dioceses) still in what is, for the Church as a whole, a fruitful relationship of tension? Perhaps too many religious orders (or at any rate a great number of individual religious houses) are much too firmly ordered by pastoral plans in whose elaboration they themselves had hardly any share? And are not most religious orders happy to be able to occupy as many posts as possible in diocesan planning offices and to have the closest possible contractual ties affecting their work formed between them and the dioceses (which in any case are considered economically sounder than the religious communities)? But do not the dioceses inevitably take advantage of the religious orders' growing economic dependence in the sense of that strategy of adaptation?

I do not want thoughtlessly to exaggerate the actual difficulties in which religious orders find themselves today. And there is also a difference between putting up with the unavoidable for the moment and setting it up as the ideal. Nor in any way are these questions intended artificially to produce or dramatize oppositions within the Church. Nevertheless, the levelling down of the religious orders to conform with the institutional Church cannot be in the interest of the Church as a whole. Nor can it be in the interest of the religious orders. They above all will pay for it with a growing loss of meaning and will more and more be given the receipt for this by those who follow after — or perhaps do not.

2 The charismatic art of dying

Part of a formal definition of the essential nature of religious orders is certainly the fact that they are institutions resulting from the activity of the Spirit: that they are charismatic signs in the Church. I do not here want to provide the theological basis for this definition in greater detail — there is surely no need for this kind of attempt to provide a theological basis and justification — but only to draw from it one particular consequence which in individual cases can have practical significance for the religious orders.

I always have the impression that the individual religious orders or even the individual provinces within each order strive at their own level and for themselves alone to imitate that invincibility, that impregnability, that is promised only to the Church as a whole. Do not the individual religious orders secretly count on the sustaining presence of the Spirit of God, each for itself, in the same way as in the case of the entire Church? But what is true of God's Spirit at work within his Church is that he blows not only when and where he wills but for as long as he wills. Surely this means that institutions within the Church that have been brought into existence by the work of the Spirit must start from the presupposition that they do not enjoy this support for ever. Must they not take the possibility into account, precisely because they have their origin in the work of the Spirit, that they may die and become extinct?

In the history of the Church, God's Spirit does not work according to the principle *Vae victis*, woe to the vanquished. It does not operate at all in keeping with the principle whereby for the most part we judge the meaning and progress of a secular history conceived in evolutionary terms. The fact that a movement disappears, that it dies, that it is as it were pensioned off and overtaken, indeed that it becomes forgotten, does not say anything against its having had its origin in the work of the Spirit.

Finally these charismatic institutions and movements ought in a positive sense themselves to exhaust themselves and to abolish themselves. Where they do not take this into account and cling desperately to a no longer relevant mission, the effect is of course that they easily give the appearance of having come to the end of their useful lives in a negative sense, and of being on the scrapheap. Loyalty then not infrequently takes on the lineaments of necrophilia: of shutting oneself up in dead patterns of life and behaviour, patterns perhaps that have been worn to death in the power of the Spirit. An atmosphere of death spreads out, an atmosphere which is certainly infected with fear and anxiety but hardly with hope and in which there finally thrives hardly anything other than painfully concealed despair and unacknowledged hatred.

In our religious orders there should be something like an *ars moriendi*, an art of dying, a preparation for death, and this not as an expression of resignation but as a living sign of the Spirit who teaches the ability to let go by means of the renunciations of the evangelical counsels and as it were as a precondition of their realization. What is concerned is the art of being able to come to an end and die, not only individually but as it were collectively, as an establishment. (And perhaps from time to time in this *ars moriendi* there is realized something of the religious orders' strategy whereby they disentangle themselves from being too quickly integrated into and adapted to fit the institutional Church.) Whether a community dies or simply dies out does not seem to me in any way to be the same. This *ars moriendi* could indeed produce a freedom and determination that in their turn would become a charismatic witness within and on behalf of the Church. This would not be a demonstration of the stoic art of calmly committing oneself to an unavoidable end (though if possible after a privileged and fulfilled life), but a vivid exemplification of the truth that someone who dies and perishes is not thereby wrong. This downright anti-stoic *ars moriendi* could also radiate its influence in an age that hardly controls any longer the ability to die and that has long since repressed — that is, secretly made an absolute of — death.

So we should talk not only of the gift of the Spirit of renewal and of breathing new life into things — though of course there is always plenty to be said about this — but of the gift of the Spirit of this *ars moriendi*. Presumably there is the *ars vivendi*, the art of living, the art of making a radically new start, but apparently not without the practice of this *ars moriendi*. For it is through this that what is genuinely new and turns the critical corner first comes into view, should it need to appear again. And it is this that teaches how to make room for other initiatives and institutions of the Spirit, in case this element that is new no longer appears in its own history. In every case there is reflected in this *ars moriendi* (to a greater extent than in a profoundly frightened or joylessly obstinate occupation with one's own survival) loyalty and faithfulness to the original cause and mission of a charismatic movement which was able to risk doing what was unusual and dangerous — ultimately because from the outset it was ready to die again. Is it not above all the conservative delusion that opposes this charismatic *ars moriendi* and thus spreads abroad that grey area of being able neither to live nor to die — inasmuch as it almost automatically claims, as pointed out above, the invincibility promised to the Church as a whole for all forms of life that have grown up within the Church?

There are many conclusions to be drawn from this idea. There is for example the difficult question whether in every situation a community should go on enrolling young people and placing them under an obligation to it without considering whether this will not impede the working of the Spirit. In more concrete terms therefore there is the question whether what really matters for a community in a particular situation, or what should really matter, is for it to accept someone or other who first approaches it and to seek unconditionally to hold on to him or her; or whether it should not from the start ungrudgingly refer him or her to other movements and communities: where possible, to help launch new religious initiatives (before he or she, as not infrequently happens, gives up the attempt, and in fact for ever). This would of course presuppose among other things much closer mutual contact between the individual religious orders and religious movements and their initiatives (among which the exercise of the *ars moriendi*, of consciously making way for others, would be included) than in fact is the case. But here I begin to become involved in the hypothetical. I would therefore like to leave this idea of the charismatic *ars moriendi* at this general level, with the request that it should not be interpreted as an expression of defeatism or even of indifference to the fate of individual religious communities — and not at all of course of the people composing and sustaining them — but rather as an attempt to take seriously in all its aspects and implications, and I mean all, the idea of religious orders as institutions and movements that are brought into being and sustained by the charismatic operation of the Spirit.

3 Following Christ as a criterion of identity and faithfulness

Finally I should like to touch on a classic definition of the essential nature of the religious life that concerns its content. What I have in mind is the definition explicitly stressed by the Second Vatican Council in its decree on the appropriate renewal of the religious life, when the following and imitation of Christ is set before us as the determining occupation and pattern of life of the religious orders (section 2): 'Since the fundamental norm of the religious life is a following of Christ as proposed by the gospel, such is to be regarded by all communities as their supreme law'. It is not yet the place to comment on this statement in itself and to bring it into connexion with that duty of following Christ which radically characterizes the whole business of being a Christian, and which the following of Christ as lived out by the religious orders always stands in relation to. The following of Christ demanded of all Christians is not some kind of reduced and tempered, and as it were watered down form of that following of Christ that should be practised by the religious orders.

The way in which the religious orders live out the following and imitation of Christ in practice is at the service of the realization and witness of following Christ in general. All this will be dealt with in greater detail in the sections that follow. What I am primarily concerned with here is an implication of this description of the essential nature of the religious life for the religious orders' understanding of themselves in this age.

Certainly the starting-point for each religious order's identification of itself is that it narrates its own history.[3] And certainly in this the history of its foundation plays a special normative rôle. But the actual history of the foundation of religious orders remains in itself an open history; it is not a supreme law and unalterable norm that cannot be revised or corrected; to use a distinction current in theology, it is in itself not the *norma normans* but the *norma normata* of the life of the religious orders. The standard by which everything is measured, including the way in which the order was founded and the extent to which it has remained faithful to its foundation throughout the transformations of its history, is the law of following Christ — with those special emphases that marked each particular order's foundation.

The authentic history of the religious life is therefore in any case the history of following Christ. But because following Christ is something other than a mere imitation of Christ that is not related to the historical situation, inasmuch as the changing situation and the challenges and demands that arise from it become involved in this following of Christ, new chapters have to be written in the history of the religious life. And in these new chapters the story of each order's foundation is not simply repeated but continued: new episodes are added, and they can develop the power to guide and establish a norm for the religious community — if they are examples of following Christ and take effect.

In discussions about the identity of religious orders and their faithfulness to their original inspiration there not infrequently comes into play a confusion analogous to that which I indicated earlier in commenting on religious orders as movements brought into being by the work of the Spirit. Just as the danger continually appears of religious orders unconsciously transferring to themselves the invincibility promised to the Church as a whole, so in this case the danger is not infrequently met of religious orders regarding the details of their foundation that are binding on them and determine their pattern of life as being as concluded and irreversible as the history of revelation itself. Yet this secret canonization and over-legitimization of an order's origins threaten its living faithfulness to those origins and to the intentions behind the order's foundation.

The question how a religious order remains faithful to the purpose for which it was founded can never simply be put and answered in purely immanent terms (possibly only with regard to literal faithfulness towards the original formulations of a particular way of life and spirituality). It must continually be discussed with regard to changed situations and demands, with regard to the 'signs of the times'. It must be guided by that question to which no *a priori* answer can be given: how does a religious community today, as a community, succeed in achieving that radical following of Christ that was to be found at its origin and inspired it?

Changes of course and alterations of attitude are not excluded here. To put it a little too neatly, and not without the risk of misunderstanding: religious orders should and must be conservative in as much as they persevere in the law of the radical following of Christ; they should and must be progressive in as much as they continually scrutinize their way of life and their traditions by the touchstone of following Christ. This demands an ability to listen to and learn from what is happening outside, with regard to new demands and new experiences. Did not Dominic recommend his friends to try to live like the heretics and to teach like the Church? But all this requires an internal power of revision and integration: above all in those cases where religious communities have grown into over-complex institutions and now find it only too easy to elevate into a criterion of identity the emphasis and the internal regulations of their form of organization.

When the history of the religious life is understood as a collective biography, as the family chronicle of a community engaged in following Christ, then this history itself has a theological status. In this history of following Christ there is recounted a portion of that practical knowledge concerning Jesus the Christ that belongs to the heart of christology. Of this I shall have more to say later.

For the moment I only want to draw attention to the fact that when religious orders conceive their identity in the sense of an open history of following Christ, they obtain decisive significance for the Church as a whole and bring their own religious life into the perspective of the entire Church. This understanding of their identity and their faithfulness towards their own origins does prohibit them from withdrawing into an ecclesiastical and social nature reserve and (if possible, by appealing to literal faithfulness to traditional patterns of life) cultivating an escapist idyll — in the midst of an age when the life of the Church is fatally threatened.

Everything I said earlier about the necessary antagonism between religious orders and the institutional church would be fundamentally misunderstood if it were interpreted in the sense of the religious orders remaining aloof and cut off in this way from the fate of the institutional Church. If the religious orders understand their own identity and continuity in the sense of an un-self-contained family history marked by the demand of living out the following of Christ, then they always intervene in the life of the Church as a whole and remind this Church, emphatically and in an openly radical way, of that law of following Christ under which it indispensably stands and by means of which it must renew itself.

II The time is now

II The time is now

Before coming to the religious life as a radical following of Christ and to describe the evangelical counsels of poverty, celibacy and obedience as forms of training for a pattern of life that has such important consequences for the Church as a whole, I shall deal briefly with the fundamental significance and historical status of following Christ. I shall say something about: *(1)* the special importance of following Christ for our contemporary ecclesiastical situation; *(2)* the christological significance of following Christ; and *(3)* the structure of following Christ which characterizes the living out of the following of Christ according to the evangelical counsels, and on the basis of which the following of Christ is able to exert a profound influence on our ecclesiastical and social life.

1 The time for following Christ?

The German Synod's resolution *Our hope* is character-ized by two intentions that provide a yardstick for the reflections that follow.

First, there is concern that there should be a persistent link between criticism of society and the Church's self-criticism. We need no 'self-defence that will not listen to reason, but a critical presentation of itself' (I: Introduction). The source of this self-critical attitude is explicitly named: 'If we turn a critical eye on ourselves, it is not because we are paying homage to a fashionable spirit of criticism but because we do not wish to diminish the magnitude and impregnability of our hope. As Christians our hope does not rest in ourselves, and hence we do not need continually to see only half the picture in looking at our contemporary surroundings and at our own history and to display only the sunny side, as do ideologies that have no other hope than in themselves. In this sense readiness to undertake self-criticism is a witness of our specifically Christian hope, which continually guides the Church towards an active examination of its conscience' (II:3).

Second, the crises of church life must be included in the practical account of our hope: 'The situation in which we bear witness to our hope in the community of the Church and wish to renew ourselves from it has long ceased to be that of a society characterized by religion. In the fear of an internal loss of meaning and of a growing lack of significance, our church life is placed between the danger of shutting itself off in a special religious world out of a spirit of faint-heartedness or even of élitism, and the danger of over-adaptation to a world on whose definition and formation it hardly exerts any more influence. The path of our hope and of our renewal as a Church must lead us through the midst of this world — with its experiences and its memories, its indifference and its calculated benevolence towards the Church, and its condemnation of the Church as some kind of anti-emancipatory survival in our society: a relic in which it is claimed knowledge and productive curiosity are suppressed and interest in freedom and justice is merely stimulated' (II:1).

The synod document to which I refer points to a

religious identity crisis 'among the people themselves' and to 'helpless isolation, indifference and silent falling away'; to the fact that for too many today religion is no longer even a private affair, that too many do not any longer even doubt; that the Church 'daily comes up against the suspicion that it is only with outmoded and worn-out words and procedures that Christianity answers the questions and anxieties, the conflicts and hopes of our world, the painfully concealed meaninglessness of our mortal life and of our public and private suffering and misery'.

The situation of religious crisis indicated here should not be underestimated. No attempt should be made in the fashion of old-style apologetics to diminish and belittle the internal level of resistance to the Church. While many people for the most part pass over this resistance and these difficulties in silence, sometimes they express them − rarely in a spirit of aggression or cynicism, more often in a spirit of sadness, of resignation and impotence, and with a tinge of despair or with an attitude of indifference. This resistance often has its roots in the depths of a largely emotional suspicion that even the mysteries themselves have been used up and worn out; that religion itself no longer brings any' consolation; and that its promises have burned themselves out − just like two people coming to the conclusion that the mystery of their love is dead. If one cannot share this view, then at least one owes those whose view it is and who suffer as a result the solidarity of paying attention and listening to the radicality of their fears about meaning and to the level of their despair about religion.

Today, in the West, are we not perhaps observing for the first time the disappearance of interiorized convictions of belief among broad sections of the population? Is there not in all classes − perhaps today for the first time — besides the much quoted inability to mourn something like a growing inability to let oneself be consoled: that is, a growing inability in the face of meaninglessness that keeps on breaking in to pierce through the failing explanatory models of an everyday awareness organized on fully rational and efficient lines, and to reach back to an unshakable confidence in salvation?

Precisely in order to stop speaking and acting in a way that ignores the lack of practical meaning felt by individuals and by itself, the Church must keep in view the dangers and the possibilities of such a situation. Even if no quick or easy answers appear, no one should act as if those difficulties did not exist. They are, of course, difficulties which are not to be overcome by raising the organizational and structural level of the Church's resources.

How does the Church usually react to the situation of crisis indicated here? A shorthand description would be to say it reacts instinctively with fear and anxiety. That may seem a trivial observation to make. All the same it strikes me as important — particularly because in our western churches this instinctive fear frequently organizes and thus hides itself in an extremely complex and thoroughly efficient church administration. Much in my own church, for example, with its extremely well-disciplined administration, strikes me personally as a battle of the giants inspired by fear.

Stabilization through fear characterizes the process in which this Church of ours has been involved in recent years. In my opinion there is an enormous danger in this. For stabilization through fear lacks perspective and in addition is extremely susceptible to crisis. Unlike hope, fear seeks to endure the demands made on it with closed eyes, wants to overcome them without entering into and passing through them, and necessarily overlooks the genuine alternatives. The whole process moreover would be for our Church not more bearable but even more questionable if those people were right who see in what they term the 'new trend' in my country something like the process of stabilization through fear at work.

In what direction does the synod document on hope point with regard to the situation of crisis I have described? It formulates a kind of basic imperative — a combined instruction and challenge. This basic imperative has as it were two sides which belong together like the two sides of a coin. On the one hand it is stressed that the Church must more decisively become a Church marked by the following of Christ. At the same time the text says that such a Church should not be a special Church for the few; that it should not frivolously just say goodbye to any form of popular or people's Church; but that it should include and at all events demand the transition from a traditional Church for the people to a living Church of the people. This obverse of the Church that seeks to follow Christ will be dealt with later, in the third chapter of this work. Here I shall begin by simply laying down the basic imperative itself: the Church must more decisively turn itself into a Church that follows Christ. In this sense today is for the Church the hour for following Christ.

The synod document explicitly acknowledges this consequence. It says: 'The crisis of church life is based in the final analysis not on the difficulties of adaptation with regard to our life today and our attitudes to life, but on the difficulties of adaptation with regard to him in whom our hope has its roots and from whose being it draws its heights and its depths, its way and its future: Jesus Christ with his message of the kingdom of God. Perhaps in our life and behaviour we have to too great an extent adapted him to ourselves, watched his spirit like an unprotected fire lest it blaze up too fiercely. Have we not in the midst of too much fearfulness and routine let the heart's enthusiasm go to sleep and called forth dangerous choices: Jesus, Yes — the Church, No? Why does he have a more modern and up-to-date effect than we, his Church? The rule for our renewal of the Church must be that we start by overcoming the difficulties of assimilating ourselves to him who is our point of reference and departure and in whom we live, and that we enter more persistently upon the business of following him in order to reduce the distance between him and us and to bring to life the fact that our fate is inextricably linked with him' (II:3). The way out of the crisis is the way of following and imitating Christ.

Following Christ must not be interpreted merely as a bourgeois surrogate of itself: in other words, included among the dominant ideas of what is feasible and interpreted according to trusted patterns of feasible behaviour. To follow Jesus means ultimately not only to admire him, to take him as a model, as can still be said by a moderate bourgeois-liberal theology, in order to keep oneself unharmed, but something more radical and more dangerous: putting him on, putting Christ on (cf. Rom. 13:14). On this Kierkegaard writes: 'Just as the expression he uses of his teaching, that it is food, is the strongest expression for appropriation, so the expression of putting on Christ is the strongest expression that the resembling must be according to the highest possible criterion . . . You are to put on Christ . . . put him on, as when someone who looks strikingly like another not only tries to resemble him but *re-presents* him. Christ *gives* you his clothing . . . and asks you to *re-present* him'.[1]

This following of Christ is of decisive importance for overcoming the difficulty which we can easily call credibility problem number one for Christianity and the

Church in our age. It is a problem served up every day to the Church and to its theology in various forms of criticism of religion and of ideology and which has long since become popular in some such form as the slogan quoted above 'Jesus, Yes — the Church, No'. What is involved is the suspicion (often at a pre-argumentative level of awareness) that the later Church has lost hold of its living identity with Jesus; that it has long since stripped off its quality of being patterned on Christ; and that many of Jesus' aims have long since been success-fully inherited by other historical movements. This suspicion cannot simply be refuted by a better, more subtle interpretation of the Church's conduct, nor by an even more learned system of hermeneutics and yet more critical reconstruction of its own history, but ultimately only by proof of the Spirit and its power in consistent following of Christ, and thus by being modelled and formed on and in Christ.

Memories of the Church's failure, the disappointments it has created at a very deep level among individuals and among whole groups and classes of people, cannot be overcome and disposed of simply by a declaration or statement. Even someone who in the long run should be right in historical detail as against collective memories of suffering is not yet justified with regard to them.

This complexity of the Church's credibility problem also forces us to concentrate on the practical aspects of following Christ if we do not want to risk indifference and silent apostasy and if we do not want to stand idly by while people inwardly distance themselves more and more from the Church; and if we do not let ourselves be taken in by the fact that passionate opposition to the Church is dying away in our society, that the polemical note is less and less to be heard in criticism while room is made rather for a certain benevolence — a benevolence that very often has the features of that easily disconcerted

35

sick-room politeness with which one encounters hope-
less cases.

So in a special sense today is the hour for following
Christ, the hour in which Christians must become more
radical, must collect themselves by going back to their
roots. Hence in its third section the synod document
talks explicitly and in detail of the various ways towards
following Christ. What should become visible is the
extent to which the imperatives of following Christ —
the imperatives of obedience, of poverty, of freedom, of
joy — can affect the pattern of the Church's life and the
extent to which this following of Christ sends the
Church in fact along ways that today it is hardly thought
capable of any longer. Finally the Church must continually put up with being measured by the standard of
the Gospel and thus by the criteria of a living following
of Christ. It cannot base itself on its claim to Jesus
Christ and at the same time excuse its failure with
reference to the ordinary human condition.

It is in this context that we must start talking about
the religious orders. Of course, following Christ is not a
privilege of theirs. It is something every Christian is
called to do. But the present situation of our Church
needs something like a shock to push it in that direction.
Where should this radical impetus come from if not from
the religious orders? Here in my view is to be found
their decisive task in and for the Church today — and a
belated test of their resources. In this the radical nature
of their attempt to follow Christ, if my view is right,
must be expressed less in exclusive forms of ecclesiastical
life (that anyhow are hardly effective any longer as signs)
than in their becoming initiators of a more decisive
readiness to follow Christ on the part of the Church as a
whole. For the religious orders must of course guard
against becoming regarded as the 'real', and eventually as
the only, people whose business it is to follow Christ, and

hence acquiring the rôle of institutions that provide the rest of the Church with an excuse for not actively following Christ, and thus relieve it of the burden of doing so.

The temptation for the religious orders to fall for this kind of delegation of the business of following Christ is great. The mendicant orders became institutions into which one aspect of the life of the Church was diverted, relieving the average Christian of the challenge of following Christ in respect of poverty, which instead was vicariously experienced in those orders. The strict monastic orders often became institutions that provided an excuse — in this case by encouraging the idea that contemplation and mysticism were not really the affair of the ordinary Christian because there were specialized orders for that kind of thing who had vicariously dedicated their lives to mystical prayer.

Of course the Reformation division had an unfortunate effect in this area. The Catholic Church responded to Luther's impugning of the special status of the monastic life by linking the task of following Christ so closely to the religious life as to obscure the fusion of being a Christian and following Christ. On the other hand, whereas in Protestantism following Christ was emphatically declared to be the business of all Christians, its meaning either shifted towards a self-serving piety of hard work or its challenge became moderated and relativized in the course of time, but without the religious orders providing a standard to which one could appeal.

Of course, following Christ is primarily a task that involves all Christians and only subsequently the work of the religious orders, and not the other way round. Hence the living out of this task by the religious orders can and should be illuminated by a text that is not specifically directed at them but at the Christian life and the life of the Church in general. In living out the following of Christ there may be gradations and as it were divisions of labour, but certainly there is no general dispensation from trying to do so. So in my view part of the Christian mission of the religious orders consists of providing a clear reminder of this link between being a Christian and following Christ and also of continually protesting against the natural temptation to whittle down the absolute demands of following Christ: against the almost instinctive tendency to try to reach a friendly accommodation with them.[2]

This is not the place to go into the important question of different ways in which the following of Christ can be implemented in the Christian life; the question of the extent to which elements of following Christ can be completely effective in the everyday confrontation with situations of decision and risk, with the experience of crisis; the question of the extent to which following Christ can emerge as a background to everyday life, and the extent to which on the other hand there should not be something like a periodic concentration on a conscious review of one's life under the challenge of following Christ.

When following Christ is laid claim to for witnessing to and rescuing Christian identity to the extent to which I have been doing here, the reproach is quickly and almost conventionally made that here Christianity is ultimately reduced to an abstractly rigorist, joyless ethical system; that here religion is finally, and not without an admixture of Pelagianism, re-interpreted as morals, with characteristics of self-justification and self-righteousness that always under-value or ignore the effect of God's grace and the power of his Spirit, from which ultimately everything that is genuinely Christian derives its life. In order to keep within the limits I have been set, I would like to answer with a distinction Dietrich Bonhoeffer used,[3] with the distinction between cheap grace and costly grace, and with Bonhoeffer I should like to express the suspicion that the grace to which we appeal to relieve us of the burden of actually following Christ is on closer inspection no other grace than that which we have anyway, no other clemency and forgiveness than that which instinctively we exercise on ourselves: cheap grace therefore, grace without price or cost, grace that does not endow us with his spirit but instead spares us from it. Clearly there is also a cheap and a costly confidence in the power of God's Spirit, and the rediscovery of the Holy Spirit that is much talked about today, when it occurs and does not merely turn out to be an unexpected theological and ecclesiastical reflex to a new phase of interiorization in social consciousness, is found to cost our church life dear: it impels towards a more decisive following of Christ, for following Christ is the price of living grace and of the true possession of the Spirit, is, as the synod document puts it, the 'price of our orthodoxy'.

2 The christological status of following Christ

This question of following Christ is not just pastoral but in the strict sense dogmatic. Following Christ and christology belong closely together.

Christ himself is not only a supreme being worthy of worship, but also, and always, a way. Every attempt to know him, to understand him, is therefore always a journey, a following. It is only by following and imitating him that we know whom we are dealing with. Following Christ is therefore not just a subsequent application of the Church's christology to our life: the practice of following Christ is itself a central part of christology, if we do not wish to identify the Logos of this christology and of Christianity in general with the purely contemplative Logos of the Greeks, for whom ultimately Christ could only ever be foolishness. Christ must always be thought of in such a way that he is never merely thought of. Christology does not simply lecture about following Christ but feeds itself, for its own truth's sake on the practice of following Christ. Essentially it expresses a practical knowledge. In this sense every christology is subject to the primacy of practice. This one could term christological dialectic or the dialectic of following Christ. This is something other than an idealistic conceptual dialectic in which the relationship of tension between two ideas is meant to be expressed. It is a dialectic of theory and practice, a dialectic of subject and object.[4] It is by following him that we know whom we are dealing with and who saves us.

Christological knowledge is formed and handed on not primarily in the form of concepts but in accounts of following Christ. It therefore has a narrative and practical bent. A christology built up on the basis of systematic argument only keeps the object of its study in view if it does not take this kind of christological knowledge out of its context, this knowledge gained through the experience of following Christ and articulated in accounts of following Christ, but if it regards this as the genuine material for its work which it has to develop within the context of the tradition of the entire Chruch, and to protect. This it does in one way by showing how the accounts of following Christ it publicly recalls and defends are scarcely entertaining tales but to a great extent dangerous stories that ultimately demand the folly of the cross. And it does this is another way in that it, this christology based on systematic argument, is continually worked out as an open invitation and introduction to following Christ, and that it is not least through this that it retains its genuinely critical power over against Church and society.[5]

The business of following Christ has not only gone wrong and is as it were robbed of half its strength in a heterodox fashion if it is exclusively confined to subjective states of mind. All we have is an abridged form if the business of following Christ is consciously restricted to individual moral behaviour. Following Christ has a fundamental social and political element: it is at one and the same time mystical and political. If we now begin by acknowledging this double mystical and political nature of following Christ, then we can certainly say that the theology of following Christ is political christology. It is not enough to join with Kierkegaard and Bonhoeffer in exalting the imperative of following Christ in quite general terms against a christology in which Christ is interpreted in a watered-down form to become a pure idea and Christianity is an inconsequential poetry of uplift (for the comfortably off). What matters is to keep before one's eyes the connexion between the social and political conditions needed for following Christ. Then among other things we see more clearly that individual moral behaviour is in no way socially neutral or politically innocent.

In working out this kind of political christology based on the practical imperative of following Christ I see a special theological task and mission for the religious orders today. I indicated earlier that in those cases where religious orders understand and articulate their own history as the collective biography of a community engaged in following Christ they make a real contribution to the christology of the Church, because in these accounts of following Christ there is recounted a portion of that practical knowledge about Jesus the Christ that is at the core of christology itself.

One could well say that in their relationship towards the theology of the Church the religious orders have either been remarkable for providing innovation and inspiration or that they have been too reserved and indeed suspicious: in other words, that they have often remained intentionally weak in theology. This was not from a hostility in principle to theology, but from an attitude of scepticism with regard to whatever theology dominated the Church in which they did not see the critical emergency of religious and church life that they were aware of being overcome in anticipation, but systematically confirmed in its existence and given a new lease of life. In the history of the religious orders there is an abundance of examples of both kinds of attitude to the theology of the Church as a whole. I see the religious orders faced with a task of innovation with regard to the Church's contemporary theology in the conscious development of a christology that deals with following Christ, in which the mystical and political double composition and double obligation of following Christ is taken seriously.

Finally the question of the appropriate person to engage in theology is put ever more urgently today. Who is this person who should engage in the business of theology? The scholar? The professor? The preacher? The priest engaged in pastoral work? The mystic who gesticulates with his whole existence? The individual Christian making his or her life articulate before God? The follower of Christ? Or the various groups and communities that write themselves a mystical and political constitution for their life of following Christ? This question is far from having been answered.

3 The structure of following Christ

Following Christ always has a twofold structure. It has a mystical element and one that is situational, one that is practical and political. And in their radical nature the two do not work against each other but proportionately in step with each other. The radical nature of following Christ is mystical and political at one and the same time. Admittedly, political is here – intentionally – used in a more comprehensive sense: as an indication that the mystical aspect of following Christ never takes place in a vacuum; that it is not something that happens in isolation from society or apart from a particular political situation, so as to be spared the antagonisms and sufferings of the world and to be granted the ability to maintain its own innocence by not being a participant.

Following Christ ultimately possesses this double mystical and political composition because it does not express something like the individual Christian's particular ethical attitude on his or her own account and with regard to himself or herself, but because it is directed towards and centred on Jesus; because it does not follow this way or that (to ethical perfection) but ultimately his, Jesus', way to the Father. By looking at Jesus we continually guide and stimulate our following of Christ. The synod document continually refers to Jesus when it talks about approaches to following Christ. In order to let the picture of Jesus that is expected of the Church engaged in following him to emerge sharply and clearly enough, I would like here to make a comparison between the synod document and a similar passage from Hans Küng's book *On being a Christian* — a work many regard as being markedly progressive and modern.

From *On being a Christian*:[6] 'It becomes clear why he [Jesus] cannot be classified either with the ruling classes or with the political rebels, either with the moralizers or with those who have opted for silence and solitude. He belongs neither to right nor to left, nor does he simply mediate between them ... With his radical demands he infiltrates every social stratum and reaches everyone, both the grasping rich and the envious poor'.

From the German synod document *Our hope*: 'Jesus was neither a fool nor a rebel; but clearly he was mistaken for both equally. He ended by being mocked by Herod as a fool, by being handed over to the cross by his fellow-countrymen as a rebel. The person who follows and imitates him, who does not shy away from the poverty of his obedience, . . . must count on falling victim to this confusion . . . – ever again, ever increasingly'.

The synod document cannot either with the help of the usual 'both . . . and' (*et . . . et*) or with the help of a modern 'neither . . . nor' (*nec . . . nec*) be made to refer to that kind of isolation of Jesus from the practical situation that dangerously robs the following of Jesus of its tension and in any case has the effect of confirming the dominant pattern of behaviour, in church and society.[7] I hope that the tension and power that exists in the double mystical and political composition of following Christ will become clearer in the reflections that follow on the three evangelical counsels.

The only point I would like to make for the moment is this: When the double mystical and political composition of following Christ is ignored, what is eventually accepted is an understanding of following Christ that ends up by exemplifying only half of what is involved. On the one hand you have following Christ as something purely subjective, and on the other following Christ as an exclusively regulatory idea, as a purely humanistic political concept. What happens is either the reduction of following Christ to a purely social and political dimension of behaviour or its reduction to private religious spirituality. What is lost is the following of Christ in which Jesus' kind of standing up for the glory of God in the midst of the individual and social contradictions of our life is continued. The theological equivalents of such a watered-down concept of following Christ are to be found in the danger of a modern Mono-physitism which would want to find its justification in Christ without in practice following him, and in the danger of a Jesulogy which lacks the transcendent element and in which following Christ would be merely the reproduction of a current pattern of behaviour.

III The evangelical counsels

III The evangelical counsels

I shall now discuss the evangelical counsels of poverty, celibacy and obedience as essentially characteristic of the religious life and as forms of training for following Christ and approaches to it. I hope in that way to throw light on the Church as appropriate to the religious life and to radical Christianity. Of course I can do so only with extreme brevity. I have to stop short of enquiring into the internal hierarchy of the three counsels; I shall discuss them impartially in the order I have mentioned, deliberately leaving the fundamental act of obedience to the last. Among many other points the question will have to go unasked of what other evangelical counsels besides the classic three are important to the Church in its following of Christ.

1 Poverty

The synod document on *our hope* (III:2) talks about the way into poverty. The text clearly refers to the dual nature of following Christ: poverty as an aspect of following Christ displays a mystical component and a situational, practical and political one.

On the mystical element the synod document says: 'The way into following Christ inevitably leads to another form of poverty and freedom — the poverty and freedom of love, in which Jesus in the end finally "outwitted" death itself, since he no longer possessed anything that this could have robbed him of. He had given everything, for everyone. Following Christ is a summons . . . to this kind of poverty and freedom of love'. This poverty of Jesus to which following him impels us is something I have tried to describe elsewhere as 'poverty in the Spirit'.[1] It should stand as the expression for Christians not holding themselves back in fear but giving of themselves unsparingly — for his sake and moved by his love. 'Whoever seeks to gain his life will lose it, but whoever loses his life will preserve it'. This saying from Luke — which was clearly so important to the early Church that it handed it on and enjoined it in three further passages in the New Testament (cf. Matt. 10:39, 16:25, Jn 12:25) — is a saying that Jesus first of all formulates with regard to himself and then with regard to those who are to follow him: 'Whoever loses his life for my sake will find it'. This mystical poverty continually protests afresh against those who follow him bringing their lives under the tyranny of having and possessing, under the ascendancy of self-assertion whose truth is death. It impels Christians to expose and give of themselves to the bitter end; to make themselves vulnerable and open to disappointment and disillusion; to become poor in this sense in the attempt to put on his love.

It is, however, precisely because of this that this poverty, in keeping with its own inner laws, has a situational component, a practical-political component. The imperative of poverty involved in following Christ includes the assertion of a definite direction, includes an unequivocal option. The synod document brings it out clearly: 'It [following Christ] continually summons us afresh to a relationship of solidarity with the poor and the weak of the world we live in'. The reason is that 'a church community engaged in following Jesus has to put up with being despised by the wise and the powerful (cf. 1 Cor 1:18-31). But what it cannot afford to do — for the sake of this following of Christ — is to become despised by the poor and the small, by those who do not have anyone to help (cf. Jn 5:7). For it is these who are the privileged ones as far as Jesus is concerned, and they must also be the privileged ones in his Church. They above all must know that they are represented by us'. The way of following Christ that leads into poverty here leads quite unequivocally to the poor in the social and political sense: it counsels solidarity with them and with their need.

I would like to propose a definition of the evangelical counsel of poverty that characterizes its double mystical and political composition. Poverty as an evangelical virtue is a protest against the tyranny of having, of possessing and of pure self-assertion. It impels those practising it into practical solidarity with those poor whose poverty is not a matter of virtue but is their condition of life and the situation exacted of them by society.

The first point that needs to be made is that following Christ is not indifferent with regard to rich or poor, possessing or not possessing. The possessor who does not share his or her possessions cannot let matters rest on the supposition that he or she is following Christ in faith and is as it were making the act of following Christ inwardly, beyond rich and poor, in a poverty in the Spirit which he or she confuses with the equally strained and barren illusion of keeping his or her possessions as if he or she did not possess anything. The radical demand of following Christ is no aesthetic radicalism. And the Pauline idea of 'as if', if it is to be brought into harmony at all with the radical nature of following Jesus, itself demands its price. It is only he or she who gives who holds possessions as if he or she possessed nothing. The possessor, the rich man or woman who does not let himself or herself be called to account by the sufferings of others, remains in principle without consolation: he or she has had his reward. Poverty is never only a question of one's attitude of mind. If it is simply an attitude of mind it cannot be any kind of poverty in the Spirit. Why did Jesus pull all whom he called to follow him more closely out of the state of life they had enjoyed up till then? Did he not want to make it clear by this that the demands he was making did not aim just at attitudes but at a way, at a movement, at a direction that was no longer confined purely to the mental disposition of those who followed him?

It is questionable if the evangelical counsel of poverty is too hastily re-interpreted; if recurrence is continually made at once to a metaphorical or figurative sense. The ability to define on our own initiative what is meant by poverty is not something within our control. There is no more spiritual meaning of the evangelical counsel of poverty than the most literal possible.

It contains the indication of where and how poverty in the Spirit is to be practised. And if today poverty as it is lived by the religious orders is often no longer experienced as poverty at all, and is not even any longer perceived as a symbolic demand (for the reason that superimposed on the poverty of the individual religious is very often the wealth of the collective security of the religious community as a whole and the fact of its being well provided for), then taking the evangelical counsel of poverty literally shows a way: the way of standing by those who are radically poor and in misery because of the demands exacted of them by society.

These reflections on the poverty involved in following Christ are not meant to be for the umpteenth time a recommendation finally to replace piety by social commitment, mysticism by politics, spirituality by practical political concerns, and prayer by social action. That is not what the synod document is trying to say, and that is not what is meant to be happening here. Instead the attempt is to indicate the extent to which this kind of literal and socially open view of the evangelical counsel of poverty has an eminently spiritual and thus a decisive significance for the Church.

(1) Evangelical poverty and the will not to possess anything manifest in it should for a start be important because it is an effective form of resistance — perhaps the only communicable and socially tangible one — against the power of a society totally determined by need and exchange, a society dominated by the spirit of weighing everything up and out, a society in which in practice nothing is without an equivalent for which it can be exchanged, in which everything has to too great an extent been enrolled under the banner of utilitarian ends and market value and which therefore is hardly able to admit publicly any ideal of justice other than that of exchange and any humanity other than that based on utilitarian considerations. Correspondingly there can be seen in the tendency to want to understand the lack of possessions called for by evangelical poverty only in a metaphorical sense and stringently to interiorize it as poverty in the Spirit an alarming indication of the extent to which Christians too have already subordinated their social attitude to that ideal that in practice today has become the standard in all established social systems. In a society whose public concerns are so exclusively characterized by the sense of possession and which therefore tends to surrender to social indifference everything that has no exchange value, the condition of Christianity is either radical or miserable and deplorable.

The synod document *Our hope* makes an analogous

statement. It bewails and criticizes the extreme social weakening and devaluation of attitudes which have no market value, for which one literally does not get anything, which are gratuitous: attitudes like friendliness, gratefulness, love, respect for the dead, mourning, and so on. Such attitudes, from which one can hardly draw the impulse for new productive efforts, are increasingly outlawed by society. Should Christians then rob themselves of that one form of protest against the anonymous tyranny of possession that they have been given in the lack of possessions for the sake of following Christ? Instead of becoming more and more of an embarrassment even within Christianity, must not this poverty spread from the religious orders again to encroach on the whole of Christian life and on the life of the Church? Does not the hour for following Christ strike in this sense for the whole of Christendom?

(2) There is yet another sense in which it seems highly questionable to relativize the virtue of evangelical poverty and to do away with the summons to practical solidarity with those poor for whom poverty is not a virtue but the condition of their life and what is exacted of them, to do away with it by classing it as social romanticism and to deprive it of its importance in its significance for the mystical aspect of following Christ. Clearly the question of poverty can today only be adequately assessed and dealt with in the perspective of the world as a whole. The relationship between rich and poor is to be met with today in a kind of class-opposition between different regions of the world, between the rich industrial countries of the north of the globe and the poor countries of the south. This view does not in any way involve any deflection from the main point, nor does it do any damage to the religious and church aspects of the question of poverty. On the contrary: the population of the poor southern regions is for the most part

traditionally Catholic. Hence this opposition between north and south affects the universal Church and its effects are to be found penetrating it, for example in the relationship of the Church of western Europe and north America to the Church of the Latin American subcontinent. But this means that the question of poverty and the question of practical solidarity with the poor and oppressed has become an unavoidable question within the life of the Church itself. Just as the Gospel to which the Church bears witness becomes a challenge to social and political life, so this social opposition between north and south must upset and make demands upon the Church.

How does the one Church come to terms with this class opposition between the northern and southern regions of the earth when it includes both regions within itself? How do these manifest opposition agree with the living unity of the Church? How can they be brought into harmony with the Church as the one eucharistic community of the Lord, as the sign that has been raised up of eschatological unity? How does the one Church cope with the fact that in it many people, indeed whole nations live in collective darkness — as if they were not really human? These are questions that are directed at the Church as a whole, not only, indeed not even primarily at the poor churches of the south but precisely at the rich churches of the north. They are therefore our questions. And for this very reason I find it alarming when in any western Church the question of poverty is turned into a question of occasional almsgiving and is moreover played down as the luxury with which left-wing church members suspected of socialism preoccupy themselves, and when even the religious orders seem no longer rightly to know what really could be meant literally by the evangelical counsel of poverty.

When the subject of poverty as sketched out here is

turned into the question about the radical following of Christ by the religious orders, then this emphasizes the double composition of this following of Christ with its mystical and political components and the double obligation this entails, without politics and economics thoughtlessly being elevated into the goal of following Christ. Clearly the message of Jesus is already political by the mere fact that it proclaims the worth and dignity of the person and the fact that all men are independent in the sight of God. Hence those who bear witness to this Gospel must also stand up for this independence whenever it is threatened. They must not only fight so that people remain independent in the face of growing collective pressures, but so that people can be freed from misery and oppression to become independent. This is among the most pressing tasks of poverty as an evangelical virtue. It could be termed a quasi-missionary task of following Christ. It is in any case an internal church task of the first order in which the living unity and credibility of the life of the Church is at stake. On this the synod document on hope says (in the sections dealing with the different kinds of mission): 'In our service to the one Church we must not let the life of the Church in the western world give the appearance of a religion of well-being and satiety while in other parts of the world it has the effect of a popular religion for the unfortunate, whose lack of their daily bread literally excludes them from our eucharistic fellowship. Otherwise the world would see arise before its view the scandal of a church which brought together in itself the unfortunate and spectators of their misery, many sufferers and many Pontius Pilates, and called all this the one eucharistic community of the faithful, the one new people of God. The one universal Church should finally not simply reflect yet again in itself the social contrasts of our world. Otherwise it merely gives aid and assistance to those who interpret religion and the Church as only a sublimation of existing social relationships'.

My impression is that the German church, for example, can most easily settle and overcome its omissions of the past century indirectly. To put it another way, whether our church finally succeeds in for its part growing into the world of labour after this has for the most part grown out of the Church instead of growing into it depends above all on whether and to what extent our own church is honestly ready consistently to accep the challenge posed by the question of poverty in the universal Church.

(3) Finally we come to another point of fundamental significance which the evangelical counsel of poverty has for the situation of our own Church. In keeping with the fundamental assessment I have developed it is in no way a question of neglecting prayer, mysticism and spirituality in the name of a decisive following of poverty understood throughout in a literal sense. Rather is it a question of recognizing that often there is no place for these and of overcoming this lack so as in this sense to claim *stabilitas loci*, in other words by means of this summons to follow Christ to indicate a specific place for prayer, for mysticism and for spirituality. It is therefore a question of taking seriously what is demanded of those who pray by the summons to follow the way of poverty: to pray not only for the poor but with them; to be devout not only for the oppressed and those in distress but with them; to call on God not only for those who are patronized and put under the guardianship of others, at work or wherever it may be, but with them. And this with all the consequences that such a change of position brings in its train.

This indication of the place for mysticism and prayer is of especial significance today for the situation of the Church in our countries, a situation that is continually described as one of marked transition. A secret split is continually spreading between the Church and the people. Our church, it appears, may still have a relatively strong social structure but less and less does it have a people. To repeat what I have said before, it is having to cope more and more with doubts from the lower ranks, with the doubts of the people, of the simple faithful, with doubts, disappointments and indifference that by comparison carry far greater weight than the doubts of its theologians and intellectuals. A silent falling away at the roots is spreading; the identification of the people with the Church is not thriving but declining — despite all the talk of the Church as the people of God, despite the emphasis on the priesthood of all believers, and despite the adjuration of the importance of the laity in the Church, and so on.

If we do not want desperately to close our eyes to this development, if we do not want to turn into a tiny church composed of a dilettante élite or into a cowed and intimidated minority, then a task is laid on the Church in this situation of transition that the synod document explicitly states and that has already been indicated here: the task, that is, of turning more and more from being a Church for the people that seems intent on protecting and sheltering them to being a Church of the people, in other words to work towards the people (whatever that may mean in detail, at all events the people in its different social groups and classifications) learning more and more to understand itself as the agent in this Church, as the agent of its history before God. Of course in this form this is more than abstract enough and is in need of theological elucidation as well as elucidation in terms of pastoral strategy.[2]

In any case what this task involves is not a break with the people's Church but if need be a break with too popular a church. Moreover to categorize something as popular is to apply an extremely ambiguous label. It can mean the complete opposite of being on the side of the people. It can be an outworn form of the traditional feudal hostility towards the people. It can not infrequently have the effect of the put-on charm of an upper class whose real interest is to keep the people in tutelage. Jesus was not really popular in that kind of way. He was a friend of the people. He did not appeal to the people but challenged them — and summoned them out of their fears and pressures. And of course he did not have to go out of his way to show his solidarity with the poor: he was himself poor.

What does it actually mean in down-to-earth terms to make his Church more and more into a Church of the people? One thing is that people should experience and learn more and more to what an extent it is they themselves in their own lives and sufferings that the language of the Church's proclamation and prayer is all about. But one would not say that we had in fact a language of proclamation and prayer, a church-sanctioned spirituality and mysticism, in which the poor and the oppressed, the weak and the powerless could recognize themselves as the subjects of this language and its promises. Ought one then without more ado to insinuate that the language of prayer and devotion can be more or less without roots in particular persons and places and can be the same for everybody, for the poor and for the rich, for the masters and for the servants? Would not the effect of this kind of generalized language of church prayer be necessarily a loveless absorption of whole classes, and essentially the weak and powerless? And in the language of prayer as cultivated within the Church — think of the bidding prayers that are to be heard — is there not a pretty clear reflection of the views and concerns of definite social classes, mostly the middle and lower-middle class? Is it any wonder if other people are unable to recognize themselves and their own lives and sufferings in all this as free agents before God and if they have therefore long since given up praying with their Church? Will not the Church start taking an interest in these others too?

Here there are great and courageous steps to be taken. Who better to make a start than those who for the sake of the poverty inherent in their following of Christ have literally nothing to lose? Should it not be these above all who more than hitherto do not only pray for the poor but with them? Would not the Church then be able to bear a more lively and credible witness to the fact that even in an injured and oppressed life there is an invincible hope and promise that we cannot in any way explain away as a projection or as the opium of the people? And on the other hand would there not be a clear grasp, awareness and approval in the life of the Church of the realization that to fight passionately for more justice is in no way to be equated with rebellion against divinely willed order?

Who if not the religious orders would have sufficient spiritual and moral authority to remind the institutional church as a whole in a prophetic and critical way that one cannot simply repeat Jesus' promises about the weak and despised without doing anything about them and that one cannot just apply them to everyone in whatever situation you like? This danger of semantic deceit in the Church was pilloried by Kierkegaard with his habitual irony: 'A handsome court preacher, the cultured public's chosen one, steps forward in the magnificent castle church, faces a chosen group of distinguished and cultured people, and preaches movingly on the apostle's words: God chose the lowly and the despised. − And no one laughs'.[3] Of course, today the magnificence has gone, to make way as it were for the moderation of middle-class good taste. But despite this or in fact because of this does not the opinion prevail that one can proclaim Jesus' message without rooting it in a particular situation, in a state as it were of social and political innocence, without falling short of the demands it makes? Here there is need of the courage and the competence to dispel such prejudices in the Church — and not only from outside, by people who know better, onthe basis of an ideological critique, but from within, for the sake of this Church. And who would be in a position to do this? It can only be the religious orders. And they should continually be asked to do this as long as they have not made it clear that the evangelical counsel of poverty for God's sake and the sake of his Church must be understood and live quite differently today.

The radical nature what is claimed here for the poverty involved in following Christ is not disavowed or revealed as abstract by the fact that one can hardly live up to it. Forgiveness will meet those who commit themselves to it if they should fail. The criterion is that they are trying and do not give up trying. The radical nature of this poverty does not really describe a goal but a common way that discloses itself only to those who follow it, with at least enough light for the next step and with enough hope in case of failure. What matters is that where this radical attempt is made it should not be brought into suspicion as the escapism of individuals, and isolated. For if, because of the necessary conditions of the institutional Church, there is hardly such a thing as a radical Church, then there must yet be the leaven of the radicals in the Church — not as more or less helpless individuals who are ultimately pushed out on to the fringes but as communities, as those communities we call religious orders.

2 Celibacy

The synod document devotes only a short passage to celibacy for the sake of the kingdom of God. That results from the goals it has set itself. And in what follows only that will be said which emerges as a perspective for this evangelical counsel from the ideas of following Christ that have been expounded so far.

In the case of the evangelical virtue of celibacy we have to deal with a structure that is always completely twofold, made up of a pair of components, a mystical element and a situational one. The mystical element of celibacy is immediately connected with following Christ in the sense of expectation of the second coming and awareness of the parousia. Evangelical celibacy is the expression of an uncompromising concentration of longing for the day of the Lord, a concentration that is not afraid of any temptation of loneliness. What it has to do with is a state of being radically seized by and unreservedly engaged on behalf of the dominion of God that is at hand. As a way of following Christ it thus impels those caught up in it towards those who are lonely and isolated and towards those who are shut up in resignation without anything to look forward to. To attempt to define it, we can say that celibacy as an evangelical virtue is the expression of an insatiable longing for the day of the Lord. It impels towards solidarity with those unmarried people whose celibacy (that is to say, loneliness; that is to say, not having anyone) is not a virtue but their social destiny, and towards those who are shut up in lack of expectation and in resignation.

Understood among the unmarried here are not only those who against their will, from whatever circumstances of life and society, do not succeed in getting married and forming their own family circle, but also and particularly those who as a result of broken marriages and families that have come apart have been driven into a helpless isolation that lacks all sense of promise. This covers not least the old in our society, people who have no one and for whom all too often there is no longer anyone to pull them out of their desperate loneliness and isolation. But it also covers the young who often more than other age-groups suffer from the secret hopelessness and resignation that like a social disease wells up in our souls. In the closing remarks on the expectation of the second coming more will be said in greater detail on this kind of constitutional resignation and hopelessness in our society that is based on the idea of progress and formed by the idea of evolution.

With regard to the pastoral significance of all this in the narrower sense, a question from the reflections on poverty should particularly be applied here. Who turns these people cloaked in loneliness and resignation into deliberate and active agents in our church life? Who gives their sufferings a language, and indeed the language of prayer, that normally is too little a language of suffering and crisis for people with this kind of experience to be aware of being meant and addressed in their own situation? We shall only proclaim the liberating message that God loves those who are unfortunate and those who are helplessly immured in threatening absurdity or banality if we do not instinctively avoid the company of unfortunate people and do not leave on their own those who are isolated and voiceless. One must be close to them to infect them with the power of their own hope and eventually with them to lift up one's head. While I do not want to pursue any further this line of thought, which stands in a certain analogy to that concerned with poverty, there is one question which can still be raised in this context. If, in keeping with the theologically consistent interpretation of the idea of following Christ, celibacy exhibits a double structure, both mystical and political, how is it lived in a way that is so unpolitical, esoteric, uncommunicative — if not to say hostile to contact? I would like to emphasize two points of view that strike me as particularly important with regard to this evangelical counsel of celibacy.

(1) In this context celibacy for the sake of the kingdom of God is consciously not made dependent on the office and function of the priest.[4] Rather it is seen strictly within the context of following Christ and the expectation of the second coming, as the expression of an apocalyptic uncompromisingness involved in following Christ which meanwhile seems too often to have disappeared from what we call — not infrequently to make it inoffensive — eschatological existence. Everything that I shall have to say in the final chapter on the religious life as a life of hope with an apocalyptic stimulus belongs here.

(2) If the evangelical counsel of celibacy has something to do with living in hope in expectation of the second coming, must not the religious orders then claim this evangelical counsel more decisively for themselves? Surely they must press their claim to this charism — in its renewed and more radical form. Must they not see in the Church's institutionalization of celibacy for all priests a certain obfuscation of their specific and irreplaceable mission? Must not therefore perhaps the critical questioning of priestly celibacy be put forward rather by the religious orders than by what are labelled liberal critics inside and outside the Church? If the religious orders themselves were to raise the question in this way, surely that would free the subject of the obligation of celibacy, as embarrassing as it is emotionally overladen, from all kinds of false alternatives and insinuations.

3 Obedience

The German synod document on *Our hope* claims obedience as the first and decisive attitude involved in following Christ. This assessment provides the standard for the reflections that follow. Admittedly this obedience does not primarily show radical disponibility with regard to those who hold office in the Church and within the religious orders. This kind of availability must be indeed counted as a deduction from the obedience involved in following Christ and therefore should be put into practice in awareness of this subordination. It is only towards the end of my remarks that I would like to tackle this point directly and to deal with the subject of authority and following Christ. To begin with we are concerned about the mystical and political aspects of putting obedience into practice, and this twofold practical aspect provides the root from which all following of Christ draws its life and its power.

This obedience for its part has a mystical component and a situational, social-political one. Sketching out the way into the obedience of the cross the synod document begins by saying: 'The way into following Jesus always leads into that obedience with regard to the Father that throughout characterized Jesus' life and without which it would simply have remained inaccessible'. I would like to indicate how this obedience on the part of Jesus was the root of the mystical aspect of his passion.

The understanding of Jesus' suffering cannot and should not be determined comparatively. This means that for the sake of his suffering one does not need to obscure or even belittle the history of the unknown and nameless suffering in the world, the sufferings stifled by force and silenced by death, the untold victims of crucifixion and of cruelty and of gruesome tortures throughout our history, nor the silent sufferings of our present everyday world. The question of the extent of his suffering depends on the question whether one can suffer from God himself, in a way that is not transferable and cannot be compensated for by anything. Jesus' suffering was a suffering from God and his impotence in the world and the radical nature of his obedience and his assent is measured by the standard of this suffering. His cry from the cross is the cry of that God-forsaken man who for his part has never forsaken God. It is this kind of suffering that provides the point of reference for his obedience, his obedience 'unto death, even death on a cross'. In the situation of radical hopelessness and contradictoriness there stands his yes, his assent, his obedience.

This suffering as an expression of his obedience does not just epitomize solidarity in sympathetic suffering with misfortune in the world. It ultimately destroys the sublimity and nobility of powerlessly suffering love. It is not by chance that it is proclaimed and handed on to us as the suffering of a reprobate. Bonhoeffer wrote: 'It [the passion] could have been viewed as a tragedy with its own intrinsic value, dignity and honour. But in the passion Jesus is a rejected Messiah. His rejection robs the passion of its halo of glory. It must be a passion without honour'.[5] In my view this points relentlessly to the mystical aspect of Jesus' obedience. Jesus stands out against God's divinity; in the God-forsakenness of the cross he affirms a God who is yet other and otherwise than the echo of our wishes, however ardent they may be; who is yet greater and other than the answers to our questions, however hard and passionate they may be — as with Job, as finally with Jesus himself. 'God, my friends, may speak, but he does not answer', is what an old rabbi with much experience of suffering told his pupils when they were perplexed. In my view this Hasidic saying points in the direction of an image of God such as is sketched out in the obedience of Jesus.[6]

By these standards following Christ is placed in the context of his obedience. 'In prayer', the synod document says, 'we venture on this poverty [of the obedience of Jesus], the uncalculated surrender of our life to the Father'. This brief sentence derives its explosive power from the perspectives that are brought to it by the mystical aspect of Jesus' obedience. If thos who pray are seen as those who are obedient in the sense of following Christ, then it is not any cheap assent they are giving, nor are they any fawning cowards, any masochists with a yen for submission, any pious subjects. Their obedience is not the expression of feeble resignation or infantile regression; their obedience is a passionate obedience. And if prayer is seen as the language of this obedience, then it is not any language of over-affirmation, any artificial language of rejoicing isolated from all language of suffering and crisis and only too easily tipping over into the suspicion of a naiveté put on out of despair. In this language there takes place not the repression but rather the admission of fear, as in the case of Jesus in the garden of Gethsemane; it remains sunk deep into the form of night, into the experience of the destruction of the soul, of being close to despair. It is less a song of the soul than rather a cry of complaint coming up from the depths, no vague tremulous lament but a cry directed towards someone. The language of this obedience has its direction, it has and seeks ever anew its court of appeal, the hidden face of God.

Here, in the understanding of this obedience, is the parting of the ways. It is here at the latest that it becomes clear whether someone is saying God but really means utopia, something to which ultimately no one prays or cries in appeal. And it is here, in the understanding of this obedience, that following Christ can most damagingly and ultimately most easily be abused.

Is the faceless silent God of Jesus' obedience not

ultimately an unfeeling idol, a Baal, a Moloch? Is he not an intolerable tyrant of a God who reigns 'up there' in domination where our longing and our suffering have no access? Is he not a reflection and endorsement of feudal relations between lord and vassal, an anti-emancipatory survival from an archaic pattern of domination that has long since been seen through? Why does the mystical aspect of Jesus' obedience, which does not want anything to be deduced from its absolute nature and which also does not want to let itself be re-interpreted as an impotent rebellion against prevailing conditions — why does this not finally impel one into a masochism that is hostile to humanity? How does this obedience not continually poison with archaic fears and pressures the consciousness of freedom that we have painfully struggled to obtain?

In the face of such questions, one's own fears and other people's doubts, it is good to look once again at Jesus' obedience. This obedience is clearly indivisible. It characterizes his entire life. And it is from this pattern of Jesus' life that the God of this obedience must also be recognized. This criterion is taken up by the synod document, which thereby simultaneously places the obedience involved in following Christ into the perspective of the current situation and of practical politics. 'Rooted in this obedience is the friendliness towards men and women that is characteristic of Jesus, his closeness to those who have been thrust out of society and humiliated, to sinners and the lost. For the image of God that appears in the poverty of Jesus' obedience, in the complete surrender of his life to the Father, is not the image of a tyrant god who humiliates people; nor is it the image of God as an exaltation of earthly domination and authority. It is the brilliant image of God who raises up and liberates, who releases the guilty and the humili-ated into a new future full of promise and comes to meet them with the outstretched arms of his mercy and compassion'.

Following Christ in his obedience leads along the way of friendliness towards men and women, towards being close to the oppressed and humiliated, and this deprives the God of this obedience of all ambiguity. Here there can be no apathetic, unconcerned eavesdropping with one's back turned to those who suffer. The God of this obedience does not impel us towards a frenetic search for our identity, nor does he absorb our imaginative capacity for appreciating other people's suffering but rather arouses and sustains it.

On this basis let me make an attempt to define the obedience that is involved in following Christ along the lines of the definitions I have previously attempted of poverty and celibacy. Obedience as an evangelical virtue is the radical and uncalculated surrender of one's life to God the Father who raises up and liberates. It impels one to stand close to those for whom obedience is not a matter of virtue but the sign of oppression and of being placed in tutelage, and to do this in a practical way. And if there is a growing proportion between the mystical and the political aspects of the radical nature of following Christ, then the more radical the manner in which this obedience is put into practice, the more uplifting and liberating but also unsettling the effect it has within the life of the individual, of the community and of the Church. Those who practise the obedience demanded by following Christ find themselves in the position of Jesus as described by the synod document in a passage that has already been quoted: they may be neither fools nor rebels, but clearly they are mistaken for both equally.

But who will take seriously this kind of obedience that makes those who practise it look like fools and rebels — and do so with the effect of shining forth and ultimately illuminating all those within our Church? Are not here the religious orders obliged to adopt a representative role and to take a contagious lead, obliged by the radical nature of the obedience that is involved in their efforts to follow Christ? Who other than they could light warning beacons against the over-adaptation of our ecclesiastical life, against the too careless identification of the social demands made on the Church with the will of God, against too rapid a fusion of social role and religious identity, of occupation and vocation? Finally the dangers of which the synod document speaks in its section on the 'Way of obedience of the cross' must not only be discussed but averted: 'If the life of our Church follows Christ along these paths, it will encounter it own experiences of the cross. But perhaps in the ecclesiastical life of our country we have already become too firmly and immovably dovetailed into the system and concerns of the life of society in general.

Perhaps in the meantime we have already become over-adapted. Perhaps we have, in that to a considerable extent we have accepted the place and function dictated to us not simply by the will of God but by the will to self-preservation with the lack of mystery that belongs to our society centred on the necessities of life and by concern for its smooth progress. Perhaps we already give to too great an extent the appearance of a social arrangement for lulling painful disappointments, for the welcome neutralization of uncomprehended fears and for the quieting of dangerous memories and unsuitable expectations. The danger of this kind of creeping adaptation to the predominant expectations of society, the danger of the religion of the cross becoming the religion of well-being, is something we must face up to. For if we really lapse into being this, we end up by serving neither God nor man'.

The final issue to be gone into in the question of obedience is the connexion between authority and following Christ. To what extent can the religious orders raise the standard for a change in the practical self-understanding of authority in the Church and ultimately also in society?

Since religious tradition and authority are no longer accepted unquestioned and unexamined but are instead exposed to the critical spontaneity of processes of clarification and explanation, there is something like a crisis of social legitimation of authority in the Church. In a society that itself is no longer characterized by a sense of religion, ecclesiastical authority is only able to avoid having the effect of an irrational domination suspected of arbitrariness if it legitimizes itself as an authority based on competence. In this what is termed a purely cognitive competence, in other words a competence based on argument, is not enough, since an authority that is only as valid as its arguments is in any case an authority of knowledge but not a religious authority; it carries the tendency to be reduced to knowledge or recognition. But on the other hand a purely juristic competence of ecclesiastical authority, such as today in my view occupies far too prominent a place, is not enough either. What is meant by this is the assurance of the social legitimation of ecclesiastical authority by legal treaties between church and state. In this way it becomes only too easy to disguise or conceal the dwindling basis for assent to ecclesiastical authority in society by following the path of short-circuiting the relation between two wielders of legitimate power, the Church on one side and the state on the other. What strikes me as more than ever decisive is the social legitimation of ecclesiastical authority by evidence of a competence that here will briefly be termed religious competence. Legitimation by means of theological and legal competence must today come about through legitimation by means of religious competence. By this is meant the form of a charismatic authority which does not only have the authority in the social sense and bear the indications of its sovereignty but one that is an authority in its entire sense and behaviour, an authority of witness that has the power of irradiating the life of the Church and society.[7]

The criterion for this religious competence on the part of ecclesiastical authority is not something that still has to be fixed. It is instead firmly established. It is called following Christ. Religious competence springs from the radical following of Christ. The histories of religious orders and above all of their beginnings show distinguished examples of authority based on that religious competence that is nourished by the consistent following of Christ. Hence in my view the religious orders are presented with a special challenge in the face of the crisis of authority that has been sketched out above.

And to begin with this concerns themselves. The rigorous demand for subordination and obedience within the religious orders must unconditionally be seen in connexion with the ability of this kind of authority based on following Christ to spread and extend its influence. Both are inseparable; each must correspond to the other, if religious obedience is not to decline into the obedience demanded by secular work and ultimately into subjugation of a kind hostile to humanity.

But it is also from religious communities centred on following Christ that the standards must be raised for a change in the practical self-understanding of ecclesiastical authority in general. On the basis of their traditions and the charismatic authority practised within them the religious orders could offer productive models for the authority based on religious competence that is more strongly demanded in view of the crisis of social legitimation.

This kind of understanding of authority, if it were to

spread more and more throughout the life of the Church, could affect those transformations of the idea of government and domination that are demanded in our world-wide society — for the sake of a survival worthy of mankind. What is 'government' in view of the growing unification of mankind and its becoming more open to domination? Clearly our social systems of government have in no way learned to rule so that they do not continually produce exploitation and oppression. In the face of such questions and dangers those who have become obedient through following him who proclaimed the kingdom of God over against an imperialism of man over man that lacks all promise should not stand on one side in what they imagine to be a state of political innocence.

IV The second coming

IV The second coming

No doubt an objection will be made to what I have said about following Christ and the demands this puts on us of poverty, celibacy and obedience and about the consequent demands that have been made of the religious orders: that this is an exorbitant and abstract request, beyond human endurance and just unlivable. To that I can only say: Yes, that is quite right. Following Christ when understood radically, that is when grasped at the roots, is not livable − 'if the time be not shortened' or, to put it another way, 'if the Lord does not come soon'. Without the expectation of the speedy coming of the Lord, following Christ cannot be lived; and without the hope of a shortening of the time it cannot be endured. Following Christ and looking forward to the second coming belong together like the two sides of a coin. His call to follow him and our plea, 'Come, Lord Jesus', are inseparable. The testament of the early Church, which committed itself to the demands of the radical following of Christ, has a purpose in ending with the plea, 'Maranatha, come, Lord Jesus'.

Following Christ is not something that can be lived without the idea of the parousia, without looking forward to the second coming. Anyone who forgets this destroys following Christ or is engaged on silently destroying and mutilating it, since he cannot repeat actions that are always similar with the same intensity. What corresponds to following Christ is an existence based absolutely on hope: a life with an apocalyptic goad.

But surely we Christians offer the world a painful spectacle: that of people who talk about hope but really no longer look forward to anything. Is the Christian life still burdened with expectations and longings that are really part and parcel of a certain time? Do Christians — including members of religious orders — still really look forward to the end in, as it were, a state of tension? Do they look forward to an end at all — not just for themselves in the catastrophe of individual death but for the world and its time? Is a limitation and an end of time still conceivable — or has the expectation of an end of time not long since been banished to the realm of mythology, because time itself has become a homogeneous continuum free of surprise? Perhaps it has becomre mere unendingness: an empty eterntiy stretched out and dissolved by evolution in which anything and everything can happen except this one thing — that one particular second 'should become the gateway through which the Messiah of history steps'[1] and in which it therefore becomes time for time's sake.

In the interval the symbols for the understanding of time have changed. The Christian apocalyptic symbol of time coming to an abrupt end has been exchanged for the crypto-religious symbol of evolution. That has penetrated all of us in its very impenetrability, right to the last glimmer of awareness, to such an extent that we hardly notice any longer its irrational sway over us and its quasi-religious totality. To prevent a current misunderstanding, and one that is given support in church circles, I should add that it is not really the temporal symbol of revolution but that of evolution that radically contradicts the Christian apocalyptic understanding of time, and that in people's minds has bred the special form of lack of expectation, the form of resignation and apathy, that today people like to call 'rational', 'sensible' and 'pragmatic'.

I think that theology and piety long ago surrendered to the anonymous pressure of this evolutionary awareness that owes far more to Descartes and Darwin than to the Messianic awareness of time shown by the Bible. Do Christians still understand something that genuine piety has always understood, when that is still apparent, for instance in Roger Schutz's words: 'Prayer is primarily waiting: awaiting. It means letting the "Come, Lord" of the Apocalypse rise up in oneself day by day. Come for mankind, come for me myself'?[2] Is this still realized at all, let alone the idea that a person should fearfully ask himself whether the only reason the Lord does not come is perhaps because the longing for him has not been strong enough, not mystically deep enough and not politically real enough?

We have to ask whether theology has not long been able to make sense of anything and everything without an awareness of an end to time (even if the Lord does not come). For if I see things correctly, all the predominant varieties of contemporary eschatology — those hinged on the present just as much as those hinged on the future — have already successfully adjusted to an evolutionary understanding of time that is alien to them. They have accepted an understanding that compels them to make all expectation of the second coming an extremely private concern, focused on the death of the individual, and that obliges them either to think of God's future strictly without reference to time or to project it into a pattern of evolution. Surely theology long ago adopted an awareness of time that allows it to understand itself as a kind of institutionally protected permanent reflection, not stimulated by any imminent expectation of the second coming, uninterrupted by any awareness of catastrophe, hence lacking the urgency imposed both by time and by action, and appallingly scared of contact with any definite pattern of behaviour? The re-interpretation of the imminent expectation of the second coming as continual expectation and the way in which this made the political factor a matter of indifference remain an objective (if semantic) betrayal of the temporal basis of Christian hope.

There is a final problem that concerns the whole of the life of the Church. The Church seems to have the overwhelming effect of an institution that suppresses expectations that can be disappointed (the genuine ones) and replaces them with a more stable alternative: timeless, purely individual, timeless hopes. Does it not, like every other institution, function as an anti-apocalyptic establishment that in the name of proportion and balance, of feasible popular demands, has long offered the excesses and exaggerations of Christianity at reasonable prices, compounded with the course of events, without having to count on the speedy return of its Lord? Yet following Christ and the imminent expectation of his second coming belong so closely together that one cannot more or less completely cancel or surrender one of them without compromising the other and then losing it altogether.

A passionate protest is needed against the lack of expectation in our ecclesiastical and religious life. The Church needs something like an apocalyptic shock. That cannot be prescribed for it by official theological circles. Nor will it be contributed by sectarian zealots. The shock effect must be produced inside the Church by those who are open to what is outside the Church and what lies on its fringe, and who are capable of the fearless discernment of spirits: those who commit themselves so consistently to following Christ that they are forced on to the side of those who mourn in human history and human society.

The passionate expectation of the day of the Lord does not lead to an apocalyptic reverie in which all the practical demands entailed by following Christ are forgotten and evaporate. Nor does it impel one into an unthinking radicalism for which prayers of longing and expectation can only be forms of refusal or self-deception that have been shown up as such. Following Christ on the basis of imminent expectation of the second coming averts the dange of an ineffectual state of permanent reflection. The kind of following we want does not merely reflect itself but impels one towards action and forbids any postponement of following Christ. The well-known last judgment discourse of Matthew 25 — where the king separates the just from the unjust according to the criterion: 'As you did it (or did it not) to one of the least of these my brethren, you did it (or did it not) to me' — is thoroughly apocalyptic in character, since awareness of the end and of the judgment is linked in it with the idea of the necessity of active commitment to others, for 'the least of the brethren'. To live Christian hope on the basis of imminent expectation of the second coming does not mean sacrificing its social and political responsibility but the reverse: injecting the urgency imposed by time and the need to act into a responsibility that has been robbed of its tension by extending the expectation of the second coming to infinity — one that has been diluted and deferred. 'In all these experiences and encounters [in the countries of the third world] I am continually overcome by a concerned feeling of urgency', Fr Arrupe said recently. 'Do not we Christians hesitate too much and too long? Are not our plans often too long-term and do they not play safe too much? Surely we stick too readily to what is guaranteed and tested, and our courage deserts us too rapidly when we face open-ended and risk ventures. I do not want here to speak up for aimless panic. But if according to Scripture we are called on to read the signs of the times, then included in that today is essentially a feeling for the closeness of our deadlines and a readiness to act quickly'.[3] Imminent expectation of the second coming repairs hope that has been soothed and led astray by ideas of evolution. It offers hope the perspectives of expectation and time. It does not paralyze responsibility but gives it a solid foundation.

There is a possible misunderstanding here. The idea of apocalyptic has not been introduced more or less fortuitously. It is no use for filling gaps in a chain of reasoning — for example in the theology of following Christ. Nor should it ever become mere playing with theological concepts or pure speculation. Whenever it has exhausted itself in number games and advance calculations about the history of salvation it has done so because it was already worn out and degenerate. Apocalypse is and must remain the mystical counterpart of a lived political reality. What this political reality is is apparent from the history of religion and particularly the New Testament. Times of crisis, when people suffer persecution and when injustice and inhumanity have reached massive proportions, inspire and drive forward the pious and devoted towards apocalyptic longing.

Perhaps the reason why our age produces no apocalyptic prophets and apocalyptic language seems out of place is that this age and its crises, catastrophes, injustices and examples of inhumanity dispenses the sweet poison of evolutionary progress and — despite everything — the illusion of incessant growth, and thus makes everyone insensible and unreceptive to the real extent of anxiety. Apocalyptic experience is not so out of tune with the times as it can appear to most people. But what is meant by saying it is time in a time for which it will never really be time?

'It is time for it to be time. It is time', the poet Paul

Celan wrote. It is precisely this anti-evolutionary consciousness, one out of tune with the times, that the
present time calls for. And if this apocalyptic awareness
were to emerge in the religious orders, and were given a
stable form under the influence of following Christ (even
though that is hardly livable), then today would indeed
be the age, the time, the moment of the religious orders
– that would also be true in regard to the life of society
in general.

What is at the bottom of the modern awareness that
we call reasonable and practical? Is it not a special apathy
and lack of expectation that continually leads one astray
and towards successful adaptation to the status quo, to
a lack of resistance to the way of the world, to passivity
to those who set themselves up as rulers of the age?
Surely the idea of time as something evolutionary and
unnending has long since bred in people's minds a special
form of resignation that persists long after it has been
labelled 'science', 'objectivity' and 'pragmatism'? Our
modern world with its civilization based on science and
technology is not just a rational universe. Its myth is
evolution. The concealed concern of its rationality is the
fiction that time is an empty infinity without surprises.
Its eschaton is boredom and apathy. The corresponding
social signs are difficult to overlook. What we have is 'in
the West a pluralist boredom that depends on free
enterprise and in the East a monolithic boredom that
depends on orders and oppression . . . It all looks as it
does during a partial eclipse of the sun: everything is so
strangely grey, and the birds either do not sing at all or
sing differently. So something is afoot. Transcendent
reality is weak'.[4]

This menacing age is, if possible, the age of the religious
orders, the age of those whose aim it is publicly to reject
all adaptation and those who by a rigorous and uncompromising way of life try to protect themselves from

manipulation. I would in any case be disappointed if their apocalyptic protest, which is stressed to the point of having a distinctive garb, were to have declined to mere ritual and ultimately a gesture of flight from social responsibility.

It is the age of the religious orders in a peculiarly apocalyptic sense. This applies especially to the life of the Church today. The synod document *Our hope* says: 'The way of the Church is the way of lived hope. It is also the law of all church renewal. And it leads us to the only answer that ultimately we can give to all doubts and disappointments, all rejection and all indifference. Are we what we acknowledge in the witness of our hope? Is our church life characterized by the spirit and the power of this hope? A church that adapts itself to this hope is finally adapted also to the present day, and without adaptation to this hope no *aggiornamento*, however powerful it may potentially be, can help it. "The world" does not need religion to redouble its lack of hope: what it needs and is looking for, if it is doing so at all, is the counterweight, the explosive force of lived hope. And what we owe it is this: to balance the deficit of hope that is seen to be lived. In this sense the question about our responsibility to and our significance for the present is finally the same as that about our identity as Christians: are we what we acknowledge in the witness of our hope?'

Who can ensure that these words become endurable and acceptable to the people of this age who lack hope and expectation, so that they do not sound like fairy tales from the past nor like the out-of-date ideology of a Church that has adapted too well to the society in which it lives?

An age of the religious orders? This is a question that must above all be directed to the Church, which needs apocalyptic men and women who demonstrate the radical nature of Christian hope before people's eyes in a way that cannot be overlooked. They must do so not in order to relieve ordinary Christians of the burden of this radical nature but to bind the whole Church plainly to the demands of the creed it proclaims.

The synod document ends by putting things distinctly in an apocalyptic perspective that clearly emphasizes this obligation: 'All our initiatives are ultimately measured by the standard of "the one hope that belongs to your call"' (Eph 4:4). Hope does not spring out of the unknown nor impel us into what is accidental. It has its roots in Christ, and even among us Christians of the late twentieth century it demands the expectation of his second coming. It is continually turning us into people who in the middle of their historical experience and struggles lift up their heads and look towards the Messianic "day of the Lord": "Then I saw a new heaven and a new earth; . . . and I heard a great voice from the throne saying, 'Behold, the dwelling of God is with men. He will dwell with them, and they shall be his people, and God himself will be with them; he will wipe away every tear from their eyes, and death shall be no more, neither shall there be mourning nor crying nor pain any more . . .' And he who sat upon the throne said, 'Behold, I make all things new'" (Rev 21:1, 3-5)'.

Appendix
Discussion points

The following questions and theses have been extracted or adapted from the foregoing text. Their aim is to serve the discussion that a book of this kind is intended to provoke.

Thesis 1
The crisis of religious life is only secondarily a vocations crisis. It seems to be primarily a crisis of function caused by the loss of major specific tasks in the Church: tasks that to a certain extent cannot be handed over to others.

Thesis 2
In terms of function, the religious orders are productive models for the Church's training of itself for new socio-cultural situations. At the same time they have a corrective function, a kind of 'shock treatment of the Holy Spirit' for the institutional Church. They plead the radical nature of the Gospel in a Church which is in danger of over-adaptation. In this sense they are the institutionalized form of a dangerous remembrance within the Church. For the most part, they have arisen not in times when the Church is flourishing but in times when it is profoundly disorientated and unsure of itself.

Questions

Where can we find the fruitful tension that is needed today between the religious orders and the institutional Church? Where is the living antagonism between them? Where are the tensions that characterized the early history of most religious orders? Surely the religious orders in the meantime have move too far into that middle ground where everything is nicely balanced and moderate — as it were adapted to and tamed by the institutional Church? Where today do the religious orders exert a shock-effect within the Church? Where are they passionately concerned to make prophetic criticism within the Church something that counts, given that because of the way their style of life is meant to be a close imitation of Christ this is something that is not just tolerated but rather expected of them? Is there not something like a cunning strategy on the part of the institutional Church to adapt the religious orders and to remove the tension from the antagonism between them and it? Does not the growing sacerdotalization of the religious orders in recent times perhaps form part of this cunning strategy of adaptation? Is the legal exemption of the religious orders (over against the church hierarchy) still made use of at all today in the sense of a fruitful relationship of tension — fruitful, that is, for the Church as a whole? Are not many religious orders meanwhile or at any rate a great number of individual religious houses being much too firmly organized by pastoral plans in whose elaboration they themselves had hardly any share?

Thesis 3

The religious orders should feature something like an art of dying, a preparation for death: not as an expression of resignation or of a stoic coming to terms with the inevitable, but as a living sign of the Spirit. What is concerned is the art of being able to come to an end and die, not only individually but as it were collectively, as an establishment; but also being able to take leave of dead habits, customs that have lost their meaning, and rules that have grown cold. Seen in this way the art of dying is an element of the charismatic art of living. It produces a freedom and composure that themselves become once again a witness of the Spirit in the Church; it is in this way that what is new and turns the critical corner first comes into view, should it appear again. One often gets the answer that the outward forms are not so important that they need to be changed. This argument must be answered with the suspicion that something that cannot be changed any more has long since become everything.

Thesis 4
The actual history of the founding of the religious orders remains an open history. It is not a supreme law that cannot be revised or corrected, or an unalterable norm. The standard by which everything is measured, including the history of each order's foundation and loyalty to it through the vicissitudes of historical life, is the law of life of following Christ — with those special emphases given in the founding of each particular order. Changes of course and changes of position are not excluded.

Question
Is there not a danger in the religious orders that they will take their own history (with the obligations this lays upon them and the norm this provides for their way of life) as being as complete and irreversible as the history of revelation itself? Precisely this secret canonization and over-legitimization of the history of their foundation endanger active loyalty to it and what it stood for.

Thesis 5
Today, and in a special way, a time of following Christ has begun for the whole Church. The Church can no longer overcome its identity problems in a purely interpretative manner: by means, that is, of basic expositions of what it means to be a Christian.

Question
To what extent are the religious orders permeated by the awareness that today an hour of following Christ has dawned for the institutional Church itself? What weight do the symptoms of the religious and ecclesiastical crisis that I have expounded have for the initiatives undertaken by the religious orders?

Thesis 6
Following Christ is not an optional part of applying Christian belief, but the central part of christology itself. It is only by following him that we know who he is and what we are to think of him. If the religious orders understand their own identity and continuity under the challenge of actively following Christ and recount their own history as the biography of a community engaged in following Christ, they are not just handing on a piece of that practical knowledge about Jesus the Christ that belongs at the heart of every christology. They are intervening in the life of the Church as a whole and reminding this Church in an obviously radical manner of that law of following Christ under which it unavoidably stands and from which it must renew itself.

Thesis 7
Following Christ always displays a completely twofold structure. It is made up of a mystical element and of one that is situational, that is practical and political. In their radical nature these two do not grow against each

other but proportionately in step with each other. This is because following Christ is not an expression of a special ethical relationship of the individual Christian to himself or herself but because it is focused on Jesus, because it is following not any way but his way, because it is not simply emulating him or taking him as an example but is more radical and more dangerous, because it 'puts on Christ' (Rom 13:14).

Thesis 8
Where this twofold structure is disregarded, what finally comes into play is an understanding of following Christ that ends up as the decidely heterodox practice of undertaking only half of what is involved. Following Christ is seen on the one hand as a purely subjective business, and on the other as an exclusively regulatory idea, as a humanist and political concept. In the one lies the danger of a modern Monophysitism that sees in Christ only a supreme being worthy of worship, not the way. In the other is the danger of a Jesuology lacking the element of transcendence.

Thesis 9
The evangelical counsels are forms of training for following Christ and living up to the twofold mystical and political structure of that way.

(1) Poverty as an evangelical virtue is the protest against the tyranny of having, possessing, and pure self-assertion. It impels one into practical solidarity with those poor people whose poverty is not a matter of virtue but the condition of their life and the situation exacted of them by society.

(2) Celibacy as an evangelical virtue is the expression of being radically seized by the day of the Lord and longing for it in a way one cannot come to terms with. It impels one into helping solidarity with those unmarried

people whose celibacy, that is to say loneliness, that is to say not having anyone, is not a matter of virtue but their lot; it impels one towards those who are shut up in lack of expectation and in resignation.

(3) Obedience as an evangelical virtue is the radical and uncalculated surrender of one's life to God the Father who raises up and liberates. It impels one to stand close to those for whom obedience is not a matter of virtue but a sign of oppression and being placed in tutelage.

Questions
Are the religious orders passionately and integrally concerned to make the evangelical virtues count in the Church, virtues which because of the way their life is patterned on following Christ must be not merely expected but demanded of them? What radical effect on society, with a shock effective for the salvation of the institutional church, is set free by their collective renunciation of property, of the partnership of marriage and of self-determination? If any radical challenge does remain, is it only to be found among individuals and does it thereby lose its ability to characterize the religious orders and to renew the Church?

Questions for religious superiors
What is your attitude to your radicals? If you do not have any (any more): are you glad that those entering your order are once again rather unpolitical and contemplative? Have you analyzed the reasons of those leaving the order? Is their story regarded as an account of the guilt of the individual order and as an accusation? More fundamental questions: Is there not a connexion between the movement out of the religious orders and the religious orders' loss of their radical nature? If someone is already leading a semi-bourgeois and private existence cannot he or she perhaps lead it better somewhere else

(type 1, leaving the order as resignation)? Or is a radical way of life ultimately possible only outside the convent walls (type 2, leaving the order as exodus and protest)?

Thesis 10
In a society whose public concern is too exclusively characterized by the sense of possession, and which therefore tends to make a matter of social indifference everything that has no market value, Christianity has either a radical or a lamentable existence.

Questions
In the face of this situation could Christians deprive themselves of that single form of protest against the anonymous tyranny of possession that they are given in the lack of possessions for the sake of following Christ? Is evangelical poverty simply only a matter of interiorized spiritual poverty; a matter of *as if*; a matter of straining to achieve the illusion of possessing nothing? Or is its aim instead an all-embracing abandonment? The evangelical counsel of poverty has no meaning more 'spiritual' than the most literal possible.

Thesis 11
Jesus' message is already political because it proclaims the dignity of the person and every human being's rôle as an independent agent before God. Hence the witnesses to this gospel must stand up for this independence whenever it is threatened. They must stand up not only for the ability of men and women to retain their independence in the face of increasing collective pressures but for their ability to become independent from misery and oppression. This is among the most urgent tasks of poverty as an evangelical virtue.

Question

What weight for the plans of the 'missionary' orders does the class opposition have between the rich countries of the north and the poor countries of the south, an opposition that strikes through the heart of the Church because it embraces both parts of the world? Cannot the *rapprochement* that is sought by the European Church with the working class be achieved only indirectly, that is by way of a new attitude to the question of poverty in the universal Church?

Questions

If the evangelical counsel of celibacy has something to do with the life of hope lived in imminent expectation of the second coming, must the religious orders not claim this evangelical counsel for themselves more decisively? Must they not see a certain obscuring of their specific mission in the Church's institutionalization of celibacy for all priests? Surely the critical questioning of obligatory priestly celibacy must come from the religious orders rather than from 'liberal' critics inside and outside the Church?

Thesis 12

Our understanding of the obedience involved in following Christ leads to a parting of the ways. It is here at the latest that it becomes clear whether in saying 'God' someone really means utopia – to which ultimately nobody prays. Here, in the understanding of this obedience, following Christ is most susceptible to abuse – with the gravest consequences.

Thesis 13

In view of the social crisis of legitimation of church authority it is of decisive importance that this authority should show itself more persistently to be an authority based on religious competence. The criterion for this religious competence is not something at our disposal. It is following Christ.

Thesis 14
Following Christ radically (that is, grasping it by the roots) is not livable 'if the time be not shortened', 'if the Lord does not come soon'. Following Christ and looking forward to the second coming belong together like the two sides of a coin. Both his call to follow him and our plea, 'Come, Lord Jesus', are inseparable.

Thesis 15
To the modern consciousness for which time has long since become an empty endlessness stretched out to infinity, the imminent expectation of the second coming seems an enormous liberty, a myth from an archaic age. But the reinterpretation of imminent expectation into continual expectation remains an (objective) semantic betrayal of the basic temporal constitution of Christian hope. Indirectly it confirms the extent to which we Christians are ourselves exposed to the pressure of an evolutionary awareness of time.

Thesis 16
The passionate expectation of the day of the Lord does not lead to an apocalyptic reverie in which all the practical demands entailed by following Christ are forgotten. It is the temporal symbol of evolution that harms the following of Christ. The imminent expectation of the second coming on the contrary offers perspectives of expectation and time to hope that has been appeased and led astray by the idea of evolution. Into the business of following Christ it brings the pressure of time and the need to act: that is, it does not paralyze responsibility but gives it a foundation.

Thesis 17

The present age is marked by the idea of evolution. It is an age in which a unique lack of expectation prevails, leading to passivity and openness to manipulation. Therefore a new and passionate protest is needed against the putting off of the second coming. This cannot be prescribed by theologians or ordained by a synod but must be unleashed by those who devote themselves so persistently to solidarity with the poor and suffering in the world (that is, to the demands of following Christ) that this does not seem possible without a shortening of the time. If this apocalyptic awareness were to emerge in the religious orders under the influence of living out the following of Christ despite its being barely livable, then this would most assuredly be the time of the religious orders.

Notes

Chapter I

1. For this connotation of 'memory' cf. J.B. Metz, 'Zur Präsenz der Kirche in der Gesellschaft', in *Concilium* (1971), special number containing the proceedings of the Brussels Congress (not available in English), and by the same author, *Befreiendes Gedächtnis Jesu Christi* (Mainz, 1970).

2. The distinction between the institutional Church and the religious orders is not without its problems. It is not used here in a strict dogmatic sense but primarily historically and descriptively: in order to explain the actual dynamism and complexity of processes involving the Church as a whole to the extent that they can be read off from the history of the Church. Finally the distinction between the Church of the people and the Church of the religious orders has also acquired a normative character over against the Reformation. Since in the course of these reflections particular differentiations within the concept of the Church of the people will be brought to bear, this concept cannot and ought

not to be used in the description of the particular situation of the religious orders in the Church.

3. For the theological status of 'narrative' and for the idea of the Church as a 'narrative community' cf. J.B. Metz, 'A Short Apology of Narrative', in *Concilium* (May, 1973), n.s. vol. 5 no. 9, pp. 84 ff., and the same author's 'Theologie als Biographie' in *Concilium* (May, 1976; not available in English).

Chapter II

1. *Søren Kierkegaard's Journals and Papers,* edited and translated by Howard V. Hong and Edna H. Hong assisted by Gregor Malantschuk, (Bloomington & London, 1967-75), vol. 2, pp.322-3: X^2 A 255 n.d. 1849.

2. Just as in my view the religious orders must become a sign of protest within the Church against the institutional Church's coming too quickly to terms with the putting off of the second coming: cf. part four of this essay.

3. Dietrich Bonhoeffer, *The Cost of Discipleship* (London, 1964), p. 35.

4. This observation is meant only to point to the fact that a christological dialectic of discipleship can be worked out at the level of an understanding of 'dialectic' that takes into account the post-idealist situation of the problem, among other sources in Marx's critique of religion.

5. In the more recent christologies of Walter Kasper, Hans Küng and Edward Schillebeeckx, this systematic aspect of following Christ either plays no rôle at all or at least a subordinate one, even though the considerations leading to a narrative and practical christology are mentioned (as for example by Kasper in *Jesus the Christ,* London 1977), adopted (Schillebeeckx), or (half-heartedly) criticized (Küng).

6. Cf. Hans Küng, *On Being a Christian* (London, 1977), pp. 262, 270.

7. In its position paper the *Confederación Lationoamericana de Religiosos* comes to a similar conclusion: 'We know that the person who follows Jesus and his message of the kingdom of God will like him be regarded as a disturber of the peace within the prevailing conditions and will draw on himself or herself misunderstanding, hatred and accusation' (Ms Costa Rica, 1974, p. 6).

Chapter III

1. Cf. J.B. Metz, *Armut im Geiste* (Munich, 1962).

2. Cf. J.B. Metz, 'Kirche und Volk', in *Stimmen der Zeit* (December, 1974).

3. Kierkegaard, *op. cit.*, vol. 3, p. 594: X^2 A 227 n.d. 1849.

4. It is of course clear that so sharp and unequivocal a dis-

tinction can no longer be drawn between the religious life and the priesthood. In the preceding pages a critical question has already been raised in this direction under the heading of the sacerdotalization of the religious orders. From this point of view the question about the celibacy of religious takes on a yet more difficult shape. Cf. the reflections that follow under *(2)*.

5. Cf. Bonhoeffer, *op. cit.*, p. 76.

6. This understanding of obedience has far-reaching theological significance. It belongs to the context of the question of theodicy: in other words, the justification of God in the face of the suffering and misery of the world. Theology cannot 'answer' this question. Its systematic contribution consists instead in keeping it continually open, to make clear that it cannot be translated into human legal terms, and to work out a hope according to which God himself 'justifies' himself at the end of time with regard to the misery that mankind has suffered. For more detail on this cf. J.B. Metz, 'Vergebung der Sünden: Theologische Überlegungen zu einem Abschnitt aus dem Bekenntnistext der Deutschen Synode "Unsere Hoffnung"', in *Stimmen der Zeit* (February, 1977).

7. For the idea of an authority of witness – an ecclesiastical authority based on religious competence – cf. J.B. Metz, 'Kirchliche Autorität im Anspruch der Freiheitsgeschichte', in J.B. Metz, J. Moltmann & W. Oelmüller, *Kirche im Prozess der Aufklärung* (Munich-Mainz, 1970).

Chapter IV

1. The phrase is borrowed from Walter Benjamin.

2. Cf. Roger Schutz, *Ein Fest ohne Ende* (Gütersloh, 1977), p. 44.

3. From an address he gave in the Paulskirche at Frankfurt in 1976.

4. The wording is Ernst Bloch's.